Managing Successful Programmes

London: TSO

Published by TSO (The Stationery Office) and available from:

Online
www.tsoshop.co.uk

Mail, Telephone, Fax & E-mail
TSO
PO Box 29, Norwich NR3 1GN
Telephone orders/General enquiries: 0870 6005522
Fax orders: 0870 6005533
E-mail: customer.services@tso.co.uk
Textphone: 0870 240 3701

TSO Shops
123 Kingsway, London WC2B 6PQ
020 7242 6393 Fax 020 7242 6394
16 Arthur Street, Belfast BT1 4GD
028 9023 8451 Fax 028 9023 5401
71 Lothian Road, Edinburgh EH3 9AZ
0870 606 5566 Fax 0870 606 5588

TSO@Blackwell and other Accredited Agents

Published for the Office of Government Commerce under licence from the Controller of Her Majesty's Stationery Office.

First edition Crown Copyright 1999
Second edition Crown Copyright 2003

First published 2003
Eighth impression 2006

ISBN-10 0 11 330917 1
ISBN-13 978 0 11 330917 7

Printed in the United Kingdom for The Stationery Office
ID 5427951 C55 09/06 5673

Acknowledgements

During the development of this guide, OGC consulted widely for views, concerns and contributions towards the best practice material within this guide. This work developed the guidance from the earlier edition of *Managing Successful Programmes*. We would like to thank all those who contributed to this edition and, in particular, the members of the Review Panel who gave their valuable time to reviewing the material. Members of the Review Panel are:

Name	Organisation
Dick Bennett	Abbas Associates
Eddie Borup	Customer Projects Limited
Ken Bowman	Capital Notion Ltd
Steve Cant	Capita Consulting
Peter Court	Office of the e-Envoy
Alan Ferguson	AFA
Kevin Gollogly	Ministry of Defence
Martin Harris	Computacenter (UK) Ltd
Professor Anne Huff	AIM – The Management Research Initiative
Dave Hutton	Inland Revenue
John Kerry	Cornwell Management Consultants plc
Darrell King	Barclays Bank
Graeme Martin	HEDRA Limited
David Morgan	Department of Work and Pensions
Peter Osborne	PA Consulting Group
Adrian Pyne	ProgM (Programme Management Specialist Interest Group)
Geoff Reiss	The Program Management Group plc
Andrew Richards	PCL
Jeremy Rolstone	DFT
Ian Santry	Civil Service College
Matt Smith	Ministry Of Defence
John Wells	GCHQ
Des West	Bear Associates

Foreword

'Delivery' is high on the Government's agenda. I have highlighted key skill areas such as Programme and project management as priorities to achieving improved delivery capability. As part of the wide-ranging improvements we are making, I am extremely pleased to be able to introduce this revised edition of *Managing Successful Programmes*.

In the Government context, Programme Management is what the best policy makers have always done, though they might not have called it that: thinking through the end-to-end process to translate policy into delivery plans and delivery plans into desired outcomes. In a commercial context, Programme Management is being used to deliver corporate strategies for increasing market position and shareholder value.

Programme Management is a vital component in the delivery of change; whether change to public or customer services, or change within organisations. The general principles and techniques of Programme Management have been developed and applied in many different areas and for many years. They are equally applicable to the construction of buildings, or the exploitation of e-commerce, or electronic service delivery. Effective Programme Management can, for example:

- identify and ensure delivery of real benefits to the end-users of services

- make sure we take into account the views of all those who need to be consulted

- make the links and identify the interdependencies between different projects and policies

- ensure we take account of the risks following from a particular course of action and develop appropriate counter-measures and contingency plans so that we don't dodge or ignore those risks.

The original edition of this guide has been used and adopted within many organisations both within Government and across the private sector. Furthermore, the experiences and successes of those who have adopted Programme Management have provided valuable inputs to this revision.

Guidance by itself is not the total solution – it needs to work for the particular challenges we face such that the approach taken is fit for purpose. To understand and apply Programme Management, you will need training as well as the help, advice and support from experienced practitioners at all levels. In September 2002, I launched the OGC's Successful Delivery Skills programme, which includes the topic of Programme Management and covers the skill levels required of the key delivery roles.

I commend *Managing Successful Programmes* to you. If you are one of our partners in the private or voluntary sectors, you're bound to find it useful. If you work in Government, you cannot afford to ignore it.

Sir Andrew Turnbull
Cabinet Secretary

List of figures

Contents

CONTENTS

1 Introduction and overview

This Part introduces Programme Management and outlines some of the benefits of using the approach for delivering change. It also describes some of the terms used in Programme Management and discusses the application of the approach to different types of programmes.

1 Introduction

1.1 Delivering change

Change is now a way of life for all organisations. New or improved services are delivered, new processes are introduced, supplier relationships change, organisations merge and divide in response to political or market forces. Organisations strive to achieve excellence by improving practices and services, to be better prepared for the future, to make innovation possible and to encourage new ways of thinking about doing business.

Where there is major change there will be complexity and risk, and there are usually many interdependencies to manage and conflicting priorities to resolve. Programme Management is a structured framework that can help organisations deliver change.

1.2 The Programme Management framework

Delivering the right benefits and outcomes from change requires a structured framework to co-ordinate, communicate, align, manage and control the activities involved. Programme Management provides this framework, through organisation, processes, inputs and outputs, and ways of thinking. Together, these enable talented people to build the capacity and capability to deliver change and cope with its inherent complexity, risks, problems and challenges. The framework also provides a starting point for the development of appropriate skills and expertise.

Programmes are different from projects in that it is their *outcomes* that matter, not their *outputs*. Outputs are specified deliverables from projects that are delivered within time, cost and quality constraints.

Outcomes are the effects of change and form the vision for the programme. To achieve the desired outcomes, active management of the change process is needed, often including transforming behaviour, attitudes, or ways of working.

Programmes require active management of the change process. Those who fill programme roles must demonstrate the required competencies and have the necessary skills and experience to achieve the change. To support this, rewards and recognition systems should be linked to realisation of the programme's benefits.

1.3 Using Programme Management for successful delivery

Table 1.1 summarises many of the ways in which Programme Management can contribute more to successful delivery than traditional management approaches.

Appendix A provides further information relating to the benefits of using a Programme Management approach.

1.4 Some Programme Management terms explained

Many specifically defined terms, titles, words and phrases are used in Programme Management. Table 1.2 defines some of the most widely used. A complete glossary is given in Part 4.

Table 1.1 How Programme Management helps

Situation	How Programme Management helps
Where high-level policy or strategic objectives are difficult to define	To clearly specify outcomes and to break down activity into manageable chunks. Particularly important for large programmes
Where there is complexity or large-scale change	To co-ordinate activities across many specialisms, business units or organisations
Where there are design interfaces between projects	To harmonise design and preserve integrity
Where resources are scarce	To set priorities and resolve conflicts. To focus on those projects and activities that will deliver the strategic objectives
Where there is the potential for common activities or products across more than one project	To identify and exploit the opportunities for sharing
Where there is the probability of change during the running of the programme	To provide flexible information flows and facilitate top-down, well-informed decision-making so that appropriate adjustments can be made
Where there is uncertainty	To provide a framework for communication and to promote common values and shared responsibilities so as to foster collaboration from all the parties involved
Where there is the potential to deliver a series of outcomes	To realise benefits early
Where there is a requirement for overall improvement	To align and co-ordinate a range of continuous improvements to business operations and services
Where there is a high degree of risk	To manage, monitor and reduce the risk to acceptable levels without impeding the successful outcome of the programme

Table 1.2 Some Programme Management terms

Term	Description
Outcome	The resulting effects of change, normally affecting real world behaviour and/or circumstances
End goal	The ultimate objective of a programme
Capability	A service, function or operation that enables the organisation to exploit opportunities
Benefit	A measurable improvement resulting from an outcome
Programme	A portfolio of projects and activities that are co-ordinated and managed as a unit such that they achieve outcomes and realise benefits
Project	A particular way of managing activities to deliver specific outputs over a specified period and within cost, quality and resource constraints
Role	A particular set of responsibilities and accountabilities that may be allocated to one or more individuals. In some circumstances, roles may be merged together
Senior Responsible Owner	The individual who is ultimately accountable for successful delivery. This title is used extensively within the public sector for both programmes and projects. Programme Director was the title previously used for this programme-level role
Programme Manager	The role responsible for the set-up, management and operation of the programme. Typically allocated to a single individual
Business Change Manager	The role responsible for benefits management, from identification through to delivery, and ensuring the implementation and embedding of the new capabilities delivered by the projects. Typically allocated to more than one individual covering all the business areas concerned. Alternative title: 'Change Agent'

1.5 When to use a Programme Management approach

Programmes may be set up to deliver change in parts of an organisation, across the entire organisation, across more than one organisation, or in the environment in which the organisation operates. A programme may be used to deliver a range of different types of change. Figure 1.1 shows how different types of change give a different focus for the programme.

Where the change being delivered is based on the making and delivering of new facilities, the programme will tend to be led by the specification of the outputs required (Figure 1.1, top left). There will be relatively low levels of ambiguity about what the programme is to deliver. The scope will be reasonably well defined and adjusted according to circumstances.

Where the change is more focused on changing the way the organisation works (Figure 1.1, middle), the programme will tend to be led by a vision of the desired outcome and the benefits that outcome will bring. There is typically some level of ambiguity about what the changes are and how they will be delivered, but there are fairly clear levers that can be employed to achieve the vision.

Where the change is focused on changes and improvements in society (Figure 1.1, bottom right), the programme will be driven by the desired outcome but will typically be highly ambiguous and complex to define in terms of what it will involve. The scope may need to be adjusted as ambiguities are clarified.

Programme Management principles may be applied to any programme, whatever the level of its focus or the nature of its outcomes, and can provide structure and

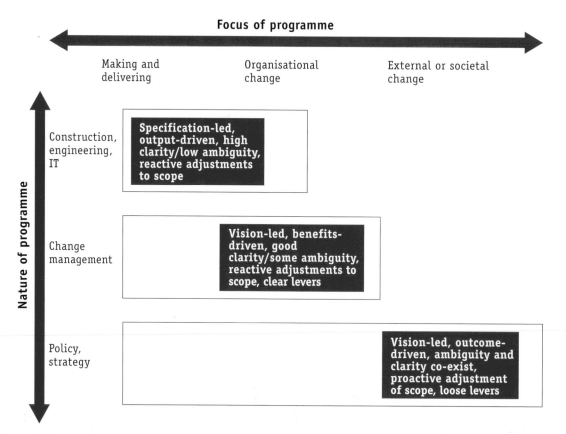

Figure 1.1 Types of change

process to all types of change. It is important to remember that using Programme Management requires resourcing, with appropriately skilled and experienced individuals, in order to take on the responsibilities and carry out the management activities involved.

1.6 About this guide

This guide describes OGC's recommended approach for managing programmes. Its purpose is to explain:

- the characteristics of programmes

- the concepts of Programme Management

- the main roles, activities, processes and products of the approach.

This guide is structured to aid navigation as shown in Table 1.3.

The approach described in this guide is not intended to be prescriptive. Circumstances will vary from organisation to organisation and from programme to programme. The best practice set out in this guide will need adaptation to suit the requirements of individual situations. However, certain principles are key to the successful management of all programmes and these are identified and discussed in this guide.

Programme Management interfaces with project management. Effective project management is a prerequisite for successful programmes. In this guide, references are made to PRINCE2, OGC's structured method for managing projects. PRINCE2 covers the project lifecycle from startup to closure and describes project organisations, process descriptions, documentation, and techniques.

Who should read this guide

This guide is intended primarily for those who are involved in the direction, management, support and delivery of programmes. It is presented as a reference manual for Programme Managers, Business Change Managers and Programme Office staff. It also provides guidance for Senior Responsible Owners, Programme Directors and those sponsoring programmes (see Chapter 3 for the definitions of these roles).

This guide will also be of interest to:

- policy and strategy developers who are initiating change and need to build links to programme delivery to ensure the policy or strategy has a feasible delivery route

- members of the executive management board of organisations who are responsible for commissioning programmes and who will be appointing Senior Responsible Owners

- business managers who are responsible for the realisation of the benefits identified within a programme

- people involved in the direction, steering or management of projects that are part of a programme

- review team leaders and members involved in assessing programmes

- people who are members of project teams or who make audit or assurance contributions to projects, if their projects are to be implemented within a programme

- management consultancies and service providers, who may be employed to support or work within a programme.

Table 1.3 Structure of *Managing Successful Programmes*

Part 1: Introduction and overview	Chapters 1 and 2	Introduction to Programme Management and a discussion of the change process
Part 2: Programme Management principles	Chapters 3 to 9	The concepts, strategies, techniques and tools that underpin programmes
Part 3: The Programme Management lifecycle	Chapters 10 to 16	The activities, inputs, outputs, decisions and responsibilities of the programme lifecycle
Part 4: Glossary and appendices		A glossary of terms and further detailed information supporting the contents of this guide

2 Managing the change process

2.1 What is business change?

In this guide, the term 'business change' is interpreted broadly, as part of the mainstream strategic management of an organisation. For example, it might mean:

- a step change in the approach to service delivery to customers, potentially including changes to business processes and working practices

- embarking on a major initiative to procure and implement facilities, services (IT or otherwise) or property

- adopting a new policy that may result in changes outside the organisation

- creating a new organisation from a merger or other restructuring

- implementing new supplier relationships or changing the supply chain

- responding to other challenges and opportunities that necessitate change.

Crucially, any of these initiatives would benefit from the application of Programme Management disciplines to deliver change.

Change programmes that are not seen as centrally important are often separated off into 'silos' and not integrated with the business of the organisation. This can alienate the rest of the organisation and inhibit the effective delivery of change.

2.2 The strategic context: drivers for change

Most organisations aim for long-term strategic goals. The strategies that take them towards those goals are designed to respond flexibly to factors that suggest new directions: 'drivers' for change.

There will be a number of drivers for change acting on the organisation. They vary in nature and urgency, from external pressures such as competitive markets or changes in policy, to internal pressures such as new working arrangements resulting from mergers or acquisitions. There will also be drivers for stability – drivers that resist change, encourage inertia, or perhaps make decisions more difficult. Figure 2.1 shows some of the drivers for change and the areas that may be affected by change.

Fulfilling the strategy and therefore responding to the drivers requires the completion of a number – preferably a small number – of programmes. The strategy sets the context for change and provides the raw material for planning, running and completing the programmes.

2.3 Starting the change process

The change process, whether in business, Government, or the voluntary sector, typically begins with a strategic initiative or policy in which the desired outcomes are already defined. These outcomes form the vision for one or more programmes. Outcomes may cover a wide range of impact areas, for example:

- individuals

- stakeholders or other organisations

- different or new services and products

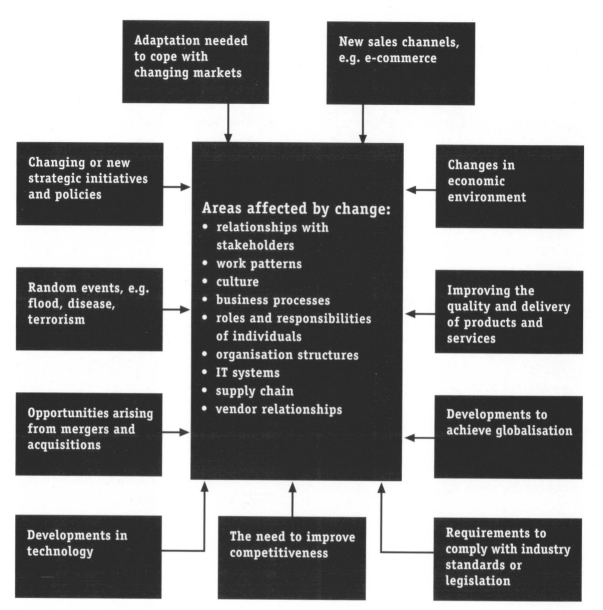

Figure 2.1 Drivers for change

- new or changed structures and operating environments.

Defining outcomes that can realistically be achieved requires consideration of how the necessary changes will be delivered. In many situations, it may be hard to perceive or understand the change in its entirety at the outset. It is vital not to overestimate the capacity and capability of the organisation to make the change happen. This will involve:

- establishing 'readiness' for change

- establishing the objectives of the change

- establishing the benefits the change will deliver

- establishing the capability to manage and deliver change

- recognising those factors that could affect, constrain, block or influence the outcome(s) of change

- understanding the interdependencies between this change and other change initiatives underway or planned

- recognising that achieving the outcome(s) will involve a substantial effort

- understanding the need to manage the change process while maintaining 'business as usual'

- accepting that everyone involved in or affected by the change must understand the implications of the desired outcomes and their ability to contribute appropriately.

The variety and pace of change in today's business environment can cause an overload of changes. A realistic assessment of the organisation's ability to change is needed before embarking on major change programmes.

2.4 What is Programme Management?

Programme Management may be defined as the co-ordinated organisation, direction and implementation of a portfolio of projects and activities that together achieve outcomes and realise benefits that are of strategic importance.

Programme Management is the delivery of change in the form of outcomes, and thus benefits. It is a framework for implementing business strategies, policies and initiatives, or large-scale change, within an overall vision of the desired outcome. It breaks things into manageable chunks (tranches) with review points for monitoring progress and assessing performance. Programme Management provides a framework that integrates and reconciles competing demands for resources, and provides a focus for projects.

Programme Management is about managing uncertainties. Uncertainties can arise when the path to achieving

the vision is not clear at the start, or when it has to deviate during the programme, or when the vision itself needs refining as work progresses. Programme Management can help to deliver outcomes while managing and controlling change in an uncertain environment.

Programme Management often involves changes to the culture, style and personality of organisations. The 'people' aspects of change must be recognised and accommodated if the programme is to succeed.

2.5 The Programme Management environment

A programme is a major undertaking for most organisations. Inevitably it will mean significant funding and substantial change for the organisation(s) and individuals involved. Figure 2.2 shows a typical environment for Programme Management. Business strategies, initiatives or policies are influenced and shaped from both the internal and the external business environment. Programmes are then defined, scoped and prioritised to implement and deliver the outcome(s) required.

Programmes, in turn, initiate, monitor and align the projects and related activities that are needed to create new products or service capabilities, or to effect changes in business operations. The projects will deliver and implement the required outputs into business operations, until, finally, the full benefits of the programme can be realised.

Even as programmes are in the process of implementing changes and improvements to their target business operations, they may need to respond to changes in strategies or accommodate new initiatives or policies. A continual process of realignment is required to ensure that the programme remains linked to strategic objectives.

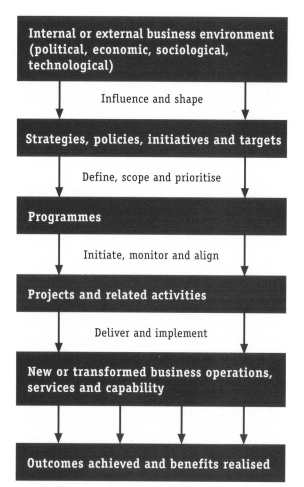

Figure 2.2 The Programme Management environment

Programme Management does not replace the need for competent project direction and management. Programmes must be underpinned by a controlled project environment of effective direction, management and delivery, and reporting disciplines that are common to all projects within the programme.

There are inherent tensions between the pressures on projects to complete on time, to the required quality and within budget, and the need to achieve the wider goals of the programme. Compromises will inevitably be required. These compromises, if they are left to individual project teams, may seriously prejudice the attainment of the wider goals and benefits of the programme. Programme Management disciplines and structures provide the framework for the adjustment and realignment that will maintain the focus on the programme's objectives.

Appendix E summarises some of the key differences between programmes and projects.

2.6 Critical success factors

A programme will involve considerable commitment in terms of resources (from a number of areas), a significant budget, lengthy timescales, potential disruption of extant projects or programmes, and major business or organisational change.

2.5.1 Programmes and projects

Delivering predetermined capability in well-defined stages (projects) typically needs to be achieved within a framework (programme) more suited to creating an environment of strategic change that is less well defined.

Programmes deal with *outcomes*; projects deal with *outputs*. Programme Management and project management are complementary approaches. During a programme lifecycle, projects are initiated, executed, and closed. Programmes provide an umbrella under which these projects can be co-ordinated. The programme integrates the projects so that it can deliver an outcome greater than the sum of its parts.

The attributes of a successful programme are:

- a clear and consistent vision of the changed business or other outcome

- a focus on benefits and the internal and external threats to their achievement

- co-ordination of a number of projects and their interdependencies in pursuit of these goals

- leadership, influence, management and direction of the transition, including handling cultural change.

These attributes should run as continuous 'strands' throughout a programme.

2.6.1 Clarity and consistency of vision

A programme typically involves significant change across many strands of business operation and potentially across more than one organisation. It may also involve change to individuals, groups or services that are outside the organisation(s). A clearly defined vision for the change will ensure there is a good understanding of what must be designed and delivered so that the desired outcomes can be achieved.

2.6.2 Benefits focus

Beneficial change is the primary objective of any programme. Managing benefits from identification through to realisation takes time, costs money, and consumes resource, but it is vital to retain an explicit, frequently revisited focus on the intended benefits of the programme so that it remains aligned with its desired outcome.

The programme's Business Case represents the balance between benefits, costs, and risks. The Business Case should be closely integrated with managing benefits, to ensure that these three factors remain in the equilibrium envisaged at the outset.

2.6.3 Co-ordination of projects

Few programmes start in a 'greenfield' situation. Other projects or programmes may well be in progress already. Some of these may be consistent with the programme vision, and some may not. Some may therefore be candidates for adoption by the programme, and some may need to be curtailed.

Successful Programme Management requires careful delineation of project boundaries and outputs, rigorous identification and management of inter-project dependencies, and a clear understanding of programme versus project responsibilities. Programme Management needs to focus on the bigger picture and should not take over the responsibilities of project management. However, clear direction should be agreed with the projects and regular reviews held to verify continual alignment to the programme objectives and plans.

2.6.4 Managing the transition

Managing the transition involves planning changes, preparing for their implementation, and then implementing them. The transition process should ensure 'business as usual' is maintained while change is happening.

Over the life of a programme, there will be many individuals and groups who have an interest or involvement in its activities, or are affected by its outcomes. These are the programme's stakeholders. Some of them will be able to participate positively in the transition to the new way of working. Others will be adversely affected by the programme or may not immediately perceive its benefits, and they will not be so keen to support change. Furthermore, some stakeholders may not be easily or directly accessible to the programme.

Whatever their positions and opinions, stakeholders need to know what is planned, why, and what they need to do to contribute. Information needs to be directed both outward, to gain support from those affected by the change, and inward, to those establishing and implementing the programme. The objectives of programme communication are:

- to maintain a high level of awareness and commitment to the programme

- to maintain consistent messages within and outside the programme

- to ensure that expectations do not become out of line with what will be delivered.

By their nature, programmes will inevitably change the way the organisation or business works, and this may include changing its culture and style. The objective throughout is to minimise 'stress' to the business by anticipating the magnitude of any change and allowing sufficient time and resource for the organisation to adapt. Some programmes may seek to change the activities or behaviour of people outside the organisation. The level of change will differ from programme to programme – from gaining new skills and knowledge across the workforce to deeper organisational change involving processes, behaviours and values.

For example, moving tasks previously run in a customer-facing environment to a more centralised operation might result in a more efficient process. However, if the movement of employees is also contemplated, then the programme will need to recognise and respond to the shift in mindset required if such a transition is to be effective. Similarly, if people previously used to working in a strongly hierarchical environment are asked to work independently, then again the programme needs to anticipate the cultural change required.

2 Programme Management principles

This Part describes the concepts, strategies, techniques, and tools that underpin the programme. It covers the following topics:

- organisation and leadership

- benefits management

- Stakeholder Management and communications

- risk management and issue resolution

- Programme Planning and control

- Business Case management

- quality management.

Each of the topics describes concepts that apply throughout the programme lifecycle and are referenced from Part 3.

3 Organisation and leadership

3.1 Introduction

Establishing the optimum organisation for a programme means defining the roles required, the responsibilities of each of these roles, and the management structures and reporting arrangements needed to deliver the programme's desired outcomes. Leadership, at all levels, is essential. Skilled and experienced individuals with clearly defined authority, accountability and responsibility are vital for leadership to be effective.

The organisation, structures and roles discussed in this guide provide the basis for effective Programme Management. They will need to be tailored to suit individual programmes.

However competent the personnel and however effective the procedures are, some things will go wrong. The unexpected will arise, and major unplanned changes may be called for. Effective leadership of a programme can only be achieved through informed decision-making and a flexible management regime. Selecting a team with a good blend of personalities and skills and a structure that lets them carry out their roles effectively will support decision-making and management. Continuity and stability of the programme organisation structure is also important to ensure that commitment to the programme is maintained.

Programme Management is most effective when issues are debated freely and risks evaluated openly. This requires a leadership style and culture that encourages the flow of information between projects and the programme level. Every opportunity to advance the programme towards its goals should be welcomed and converted into constructive progress.

3.2 Key principles of leadership

Programmes coalesce and integrate strategic objectives by translating them into concrete targets for individual projects. Leading, directing and managing a programme provides the 'bridge' between strategic objectives and projects.

The key principles for effective leadership of a programme are:

- empowered **decision-making**, giving individuals the autonomy to fulfil their roles effectively. Motivation, reward and appraisal systems are vital for fostering the attitudes and energy to drive the programme

- visible **commitment** and authority, with enough seniority to:
  - ensure the correct resources are available to the programme
  - influence and engage with stakeholders
  - balance the programme's priorities with those of the ongoing business operations
  - focus on realisation of the business benefits

- relevant **skills and experience** to provide active management of:
  - the cultural and people issues involved in change
  - the programme's finances and the inevitable conflicting demands on resources
  - the co-ordination of the projects within the

programme to the transition to new operational services while maintaining 'business as usual'

● risk identification, evaluation and management.

3.3 Programme organisation

Figure 3.1 shows the core programme roles and functions and how they relate to each other. Sections 3.4 to 3.10 describe the roles and the generic responsibilities for each, along with the skills that the individuals fulfilling them will need.

3.4 Programme sponsorship

Programme sponsorship means making the investment decision and providing top-level endorsement of the rationale and objectives for the programme. Sponsorship also means continuing senior management commitment to promoting and supporting the changes introduced by the programme, and championing the implementation of the new capabilities delivered by the

programme to ensure that the expected benefits are realised and the desired outcomes achieved.

The programme's sponsors are key stakeholders and form the Sponsoring Group for the programme.

3.5 Responsibilities of the Sponsoring Group

The Sponsoring Group represents those senior managers who are responsible for the investment decision, defining the direction of the business and establishing frameworks to achieve the desired objectives. They must take the lead in establishing the values and behaviours required by the change effort, often 'leading by example'. Without the commitment and direct involvement of senior management, a transformational change is unlikely to progress very far.

The life of a programme, and the period of transition in particular, is a time of uncertainty. Many normal procedures, reporting relationships and responsibilities may no longer apply. All members of the Sponsoring Group must take the lead in establishing a style of leadership

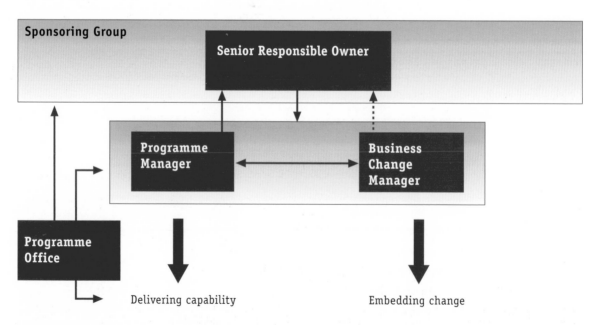

Figure 3.1 Basic programme organisation

appropriate to the organisation and the nature of the change. In most change situations there will need to be increased emphasis on motivation of staff, promotion of team-working, empowerment at all levels, encouragement of initiatives, and recognition of appropriate risk-taking.

The specific responsibilities of the Sponsoring Group will include:

- providing the Programme Mandate and investment decision

- creating an environment in which the programme can thrive

- endorsing, advising and supporting the Senior Responsible Owner

- providing continued commitment and endorsement in support of the Senior Responsible Owner at programme milestones

- approving the progress of the programme against the strategic objectives

- providing visible leadership and commitment to the programme at communication events

- confirming successful delivery and sign-off at the closure of the programme.

3.6 Programme direction

The **Senior Responsible Owner** has overall accountability for the programme, together with personal responsibility for ensuring that it meets its objectives and realises the expected benefits. The individual who fulfils this role should be a peer member of the Sponsoring Group and must be empowered to direct the programme and take decisions. They must have enough seniority and authority to provide leadership to the programme team and take on accountability for delivery.

3.7 Responsibilities of the Senior Responsible Owner

The Senior Responsible Owner is ultimately accountable for the success of the programme and is responsible for enabling the organisation to exploit the new environment resulting from the programme, meeting the new business needs and delivering new levels of performance, benefit, service delivery, value or market share. The title of 'Senior Responsible Owner' is used extensively within the UK public sector. Other titles may be used to accommodate industry or organisational styles.

The responsibilities of the Senior Responsible Owner role include:

- owning the vision for the programme and being its 'champion', providing clear leadership and direction throughout its life

- securing the investment required to set up and run the programme, and fund the transition activities so that the desired benefits are realised

- providing overall direction and leadership for the delivery and implementation of the programme, with personal accountability for its outcome (this should be an important measure of their individual performance)

- being accountable for the programme's governance arrangements by ensuring the programme, including its investment, is established and managed according to appropriate requirements and quality

- being responsible for key programme information, including the Programme Brief and the Business Case

- managing the interface with key senior stakeholders and ensuring that interfaces and communications with all stakeholders are effective

- managing the key strategic risks facing the programme

- maintaining the alignment of the programme to the organisation's strategic direction. Evolving business needs and emerging issues that impact the programme will undoubtedly arise. The Senior Responsible Owner is responsible for ensuring that such issues are addressed appropriately

- ensuring that the organisation and its staff are managed carefully through the process of change, that the results are reviewed and assessed objectively, and that adjustments are made as necessary

- commissioning and chairing reviews both during the programme and following programme closure that formally assess the programme's:

  - continued alignment with its objectives

  - capability of delivery

  - measurable achievement of benefits

- managing and supporting the Programme Manager.

3.7.1 Appointing a Senior Responsible Owner

The Senior Responsible Owner must have the seniority for the responsibilities and accountabilities the role involves. Even though they may only be involved in the day-to-day activities of the programme on a part-time basis, they must be proactive and visible as the driving force behind the programme.

Programmes require strong leadership and decision-making skills. However, different types of programme require different styles of leadership. For example, programmes involving significant internal change for staff will have different issues from those focused on external change. The appointment process should ensure that the experience, character and personality of the individual appointed to the Senior Responsible Owner role are right for the programme.

The Senior Responsible Owner needs to be able to combine realism with openness and the clarity of expression to communicate the programme's vision effectively.

In addition, the Senior Responsible Owner must:

- be able to give purpose and direction to the programme and take strategic decisions

- lead by example and focus on delivery

- build productive relationships across the programme team and have access to, and credibility with, key stakeholders.

3.8 Managing the programme and delivering change

There is a fundamental difference between the delivery of a new capability and actually realising measurable benefits as a result of using that capability. This difference is reflected in the complementary roles of Programme Manager and Business Change Manager. The Programme Manager is responsible for delivering the capability; the Business Change Manager is responsible for realising the resultant benefits by embedding that capability into business operations. The individuals appointed to each role must be able to work in close partnership to ensure that the right capabilities are delivered and that they are put to best use.

3.9 Managing the programme

The role of **Programme Manager** is responsible for leading and managing the setting up of the programme through to delivery of the new capabilities and realisation of benefits. Managing a programme is not simply a line management function overseeing the delivery of a number of projects. The Programme Manager role involves proactive interventions and decision-making to ensure that the programme stays on track.

Programmes do not usually have a clear path towards a well-defined goal. Therefore, they can rarely be managed using traditional approaches. The Programme Manager is responsible for co-ordinating and monitoring the work of the programme in an uncertain environment.

Successful delivery will depend on the effective management of issues, conflicts, priorities, communications and personnel. The Programme Manager will need the ability to work positively with the full range of individuals and groups involved in the programme.

3.10 Responsibilities of the Programme Manager

The Programme Manager is responsible, on behalf of the Senior Responsible Owner, for successful delivery of the new capability. The role requires the effective co-ordination of the projects and their interdependencies, and any risks and other issues that may arise. In most cases, the Programme Manager will typically work full-time on the programme, as the role is crucial for creating and maintaining enthusiasm.

As the programme is implemented, changes to policy, strategy, or infrastructure may have an impact right across the Project Portfolio, or outside the programme. The Programme Manager is responsible for the overall integrity and coherence of the programme, and develops and maintains the programme environment to support each individual project within it – typically through the Programme Office function.

The responsibilities of the Programme Manager role will also include the following:

- planning and designing the programme and proactively monitoring its overall progress, resolving issues and initiating corrective action as appropriate

- defining the programme's governance framework

- ensuring the integrity of the programme – focusing inwardly on the internal consistency of the programme; and outwardly on its coherence with infrastructure planning, interfaces with other programmes and corporate technical and specialist standards. This particular aspect may be allocated to a separate dedicated role (often referred to as 'business or technical design authority' or 'strategic architect') particularly on large, complex programmes

- managing the programme's budget on behalf of the Senior Responsible Owner, monitoring the expenditures and costs against benefits that are realised as the programme progresses

- facilitating the appointment of individuals to the project delivery teams

- ensuring that the delivery of new products or services from the projects meets requirements and is to the appropriate quality, on time and within budget, in accordance with the Programme Plan and programme governance arrangements

- ensuring maximum efficiency in the allocation of resources and skills within the Project Portfolio

- managing third-party contributions to the programme

- managing the communications with stakeholders

- managing the dependencies and interfaces between projects

- managing risks to the programme's successful outcome

- initiating extra activities and other management interventions wherever gaps in the programme are identified or issues arise

- reporting progress of the programme at regular intervals to the Senior Responsible Owner.

Once projects become established, the role of Programme Manager focuses on monitoring interdependencies between projects and changes within the Project Portfolio. The day-to-day management and delivery of the projects will be carried out by the designated project teams.

Throughout the programme, the Programme Manager provides the ongoing 'health check' of the programme by reassessing whether the projects continue to meet the programme's objectives and continue to use available funds and resources efficiently. This requires the timely management of exceptions, slippage and conflicting priorities.

3.10.1 Appointing the Programme Manager

The individual appointed to the role of Programme Manager must have the necessary seniority to be able to take on the responsibilities required of the role. The Programme Manager must have strong leadership and management skills, and may well have a project management background. The balance of skills required in the Programme Manager often changes as the programme develops: the person with the skills to set up a programme is not necessarily the right one to drive through its implementation.

The Programme Manager must understand the wider objectives of the programme, have credibility within the programme environment and be able to influence others. They must be able to develop and maintain effective working relationships with other members of the Programme Management Team, senior managers, the project teams and third-party service providers involved in the management and operations of the programme.

The Programme Manager should also have:

- effective leadership, interpersonal and communication skills

- the ability to command respect and to create a sense of community amongst the (often disparate) members of the project teams

- a good knowledge of techniques for planning, monitoring and controlling programmes

- a good knowledge of project management approaches such as PRINCE2

- a good knowledge of budgeting and resource allocation procedures

- sufficient seniority and credibility to advise project teams on their projects in relation to the programme

- the ability to find ways of solving or pre-empting problems.

3.11 Delivering change

The delivery of change will not happen on its own. The outputs required from projects need to be defined and targeted, based on the contribution they will make to realising benefits and achieving outcomes.

The role of **Business Change Manager** (often referred to as the 'Change Agent') has responsibility for benefits definition and management throughout the programme. More than one individual may be required to fulfil this role – exactly how many will depend on the number of business areas targeted for benefits realisation.

To realise benefits, the programme must be closely integrated with mainstream business activities. It is only when changes become 'business as usual' that the benefits will be realised. The Business Change Manager role is key to providing the 'bridge' between the programme and the business operations since the individual(s) will be an integral part of the business operations.

The Business Change Manager role represents the Senior Responsible Owner's (and hence the Sponsoring Group's) interests in the final outcome of the programme, in terms of measurable improvements in business performance.

Where substantial change in business operations is required, the individual(s) appointed to the role of Business Change Manager will be responsible for creating the new business structures, operations and working practices.

Business Change Managers should have appropriate responsibility and authority within the business areas within which change will take effect and benefits will be realised.

3.12 Responsibilities of the Business Change Manager

The role of Business Change Manager is primarily benefits-focused. The Business Change Manager role is responsible, on behalf of the Senior Responsible Owner, for defining the benefits, assessing progress towards realisation, and achieving measured improvements. This need to define and realise benefits in terms of measured improvements in business performance means that the Business Change Manager role must be 'business-side', in order to provide a bridge between the programme and business operations. This bridge between the business and the programme is represented by the dotted line relationship between the Business Change Manager and the Senior Responsible Owner in Figure 3.1.

On many programmes, change will affect different parts of the organisation. In such situations there should be a team of Business Change Managers, one for each business area.

The Business Change Manager role will include the following responsibilities:

- ensuring the interests of the Sponsoring Group are met by the programme

- obtaining assurance for the Sponsoring Group that the delivery of new capability is compatible with realisation of the benefits

- working with the Programme Manager to ensure that the work of the programme, including the scoping of each project, covers the necessary aspects required to deliver the products or services that will lead to operational benefits

- working with the Programme Manager to identify projects that will contribute to realising benefits and achieving outcomes

- identifying, defining and tracking the benefits and outcomes required of the programme

- identifying and implementing the maximum improvements in business operations (both extant and newly created) as groups of projects deliver their products or services into operational use

- managing the realisation of benefits, and ensuring that continued accrual of benefits can be achieved and measured after the programme has been completed

- establishing and implementing the mechanisms by which benefits can be realised and measured

- taking the lead on transition management; ensuring that 'business as usual' is maintained during the transition and the changes are effectively integrated into the business

- preparing the affected business areas for the transition to new ways of working; potentially implementing new business processes

- optimising the timing of the release of project deliverables into business operations.

As the programme progresses, the Business Change Manager is responsible for monitoring outcomes against what was predicted.

3.12.1 Appointing the Business Change Manager(s)

The individual, or individuals, appointed as Business Change Manager(s) should be drawn from the relevant business areas. Suitable individuals are likely to have ongoing operational responsibilities within their business areas. Their participation in the programme should be an integral part of their normal responsibilities, to enable changes resulting from the programme to be firmly embedded in the organisation.

Business Change Managers require detailed knowledge of the business environment and direct business experience. In particular, they need an understanding of the management structures, politics and culture of the organisation(s) involved in the programme. They also need management skills to co-ordinate personnel from different disciplines and with differing viewpoints. They need effective marketing and communication skills to sell the programme vision to staff at all levels of the business.

Business Change Manager(s) should also have change management skills and enough experience to be able to bring order to complex situations and maintain focus on the programme's objectives.

Knowledge of certain management techniques may also be useful, for example:

- business change techniques, such as business process re-engineering

- benefits identification, modelling and management techniques.

3.13 Supporting the programme

Programmes are major undertakings, often affecting large numbers of people and organisations and generating a substantial volume of information. The nerve centre and information hub of a programme is the **Programme Office**. All information, communication, monitoring and control activities for the programme are co-ordinated through the Programme Office.

3.14 The Programme Office

The Programme Office may be dedicated to supporting a single programme, or it may support a number of programmes. The level of resourcing for the Programme Office will vary depending on the size and capabilities of the organisation. For example, with appropriate expertise, the Programme Office may be a 'centre of excellence' for all programmes and projects within the organisation, providing specialist expertise and facilitation across the programme and its projects. In many cases, the manager of the Programme Office will also act as deputy to the Programme Manager.

The Programme Office can provide some aspects of assurance for the programme. However, it is important to have an independent assurance function in addition to any internal assurance function.

The core function of the Programme Office is to provide an information hub for the programme. This will typically involve the following:

- tracking and reporting:
  - tracking measurements
  - reporting progress
- information management (websites are useful tools for providing these facilities):
  - holding master copies of all programme information
  - generating all necessary quality management documentation
  - maintaining, controlling and updating programme documentation
  - establishing and maintaining the index to an electronic library of programme information

- financial accounting:

  - assisting the Programme Manager with budget control for the programme

  - maintaining status reports on all projects in the programme

- risk and issue tracking

  - analysing interfaces and critical dependencies between projects and recommending appropriate actions to the Programme Manager

  - maintaining the list of stakeholders and their interests

- quality control: establishing consistent practices and standards adhering to the programme governance arrangements, including project planning, reporting, change control, analysing risks and maintaining and updating the Risk Register for the programme

- change control:

  - registering changes for subsequent investigation and resolution

  - monitoring items identified as requiring action

  - prompting timely actions

  - reporting on whether required actions have been carried out.

The Programme Office may be sufficiently resourced to provide additional expertise across the programme, for example:

- providing a strategic overview of all programmes and interdependencies, and reporting upward to senior management

- providing consultancy-style support to project delivery teams at initiation and throughout the lifecycle of the programme; ensuring a common approach is adopted and sharing good practice

- carrying out health checks and advising on solutions during the lifetime of the programme and individual projects, for example, facilitating workshops involving project teams, stakeholders and members of the programme team.

3.14.1 Resourcing the Programme Office

The Programme Office should add value to the programme through the knowledge, experience and skills of its staff. The following attributes are worth considering when making Programme Office appointments:

- proven track record in programme/project management and implementation

- expertise in programme/project management methodologies and processes

- active experience in risk management

- Business Case and appraisal skills

- interpersonal skills; communication skills at all levels.

Programme Offices and Project Offices may be combined where it is a sensible use of resources to have the same team providing both functions.

3.15 Designing and implementing a programme organisation

There is no single programme organisation that will fit every type of programme. Each programme should be directed and managed with the appropriate level of management resources to facilitate clear direction setting and effective management of ongoing progress, but without incurring excessive management overheads.

The programme organisation will have to meet needs that include:

- the level of integration and overlap required with project organisations

- the need to split the responsibilities of the core programme roles across more than one individual to cope with large-scale programmes

- the requirement for building cross-organisation structures

- appropriate choice of titles for programme roles to fit with existing job titles and industry standards.

A Programme Board may be used to bring together key stakeholders, partners, or investors as part of the organisation structure. The Senior Responsible Owner would typically chair such a board.

3.15.1 Integrating project organisations

Designing the appropriate levels of engagement between the projects and the programme is a key part of establishing an effective programme organisation. Project level organisation structures need to have clear leadership, direction-setting, decision-making and management, whether they are operating within a programme or independently. There are different forms of project organisations and different ways of integrating project organisations into a programme organisation; Figure 3.2 shows some examples.

Scenario (A) – Some projects will benefit from a dedicated Project Board to provide the required level of management direction and decision-making. The Project Board should have a clear set of responsibilities, agreed at the programme level, for directing the project and defining how the project should interface with the programme. The chair of the Project Board will be the

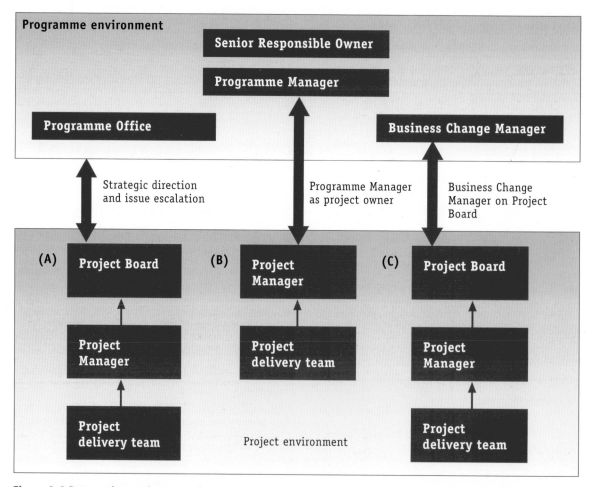

Figure 3.2 Integrating project organisations

project's Senior Responsible Owner (or Executive). This scenario may be well suited to larger projects within the Project Portfolio. It may be useful to establish a single Board to eliminate the need for multiple Project Boards.

Scenario (B) – Projects that are central to the programme may work well with the Programme Manager fulfilling the project Senior Responsible Owner role and maintaining a direct link between the project and the programme.

Scenario (C) – The Business Change Manager may provide valuable user-side input and assurance to projects within the Project Portfolio. In this scenario, the Business Change Manager may fulfil the senior user role on the Project Board.

3.15.2 Splitting programme roles

The core programme roles may need to be allocated to more than one individual, particularly on large or complex programmes. The roles selected should cover all the core programme responsibilities and provide clear boundaries of responsibility between them. Whatever structure is designed, each appointed individual should have a clearly defined set of responsibilities.

Figure 3.3 shows one example of a programme organisation structure where roles have been split to allocate specific responsibilities across additional roles. For example, the change management role in Figure 3.3 would be providing co-ordination across multiple business areas as changes are implemented.

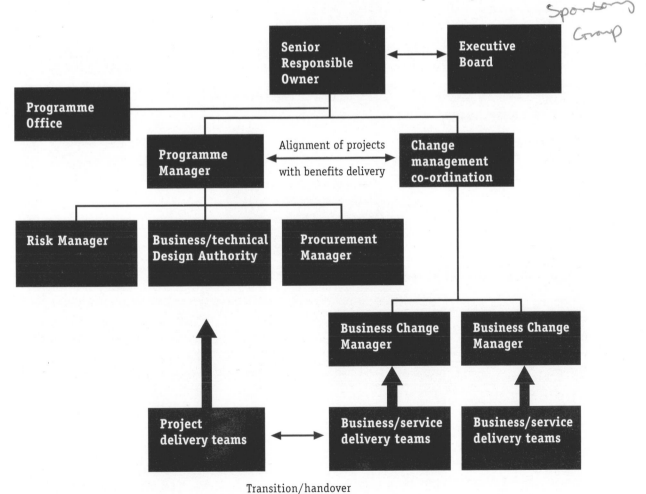

Figure 3.3 Splitting roles

3.15.3 Cross-organisational programmes

When two or more organisations come together to work on a programme, managing and directing their respective contributions can be complex. One example of cross-organisational working might be where one organisation is providing most of the funding and purchasing capital assets such as a new building and the other providing the staffing, infrastructure and systems for a new service facility. Both organisations require a return on their respective investments and so need to collaborate effectively to make the 'partnership' deliver the required outcome. Each participating organisation should have a clearly defined role that is agreed and understood by all the participating organisations.

One approach to designing an appropriate programme structure is to establish a separate entity for the purposes of co-ordinating and leading the programme. This separates the business of making the 'partnership' work from the internal priorities of each participating organisation. Figure 3.4 shows an example of a structure bringing together three organisations. The structure may be a specifically created legal entity, or it may be based on formal terms of reference or contractual agreements.

The challenges facing cross-organisational programmes are generally the same as for all major programmes. However, increased complexity can mean that different types of issue, with greater impact, can arise. Some particular aspects that present challenges are:

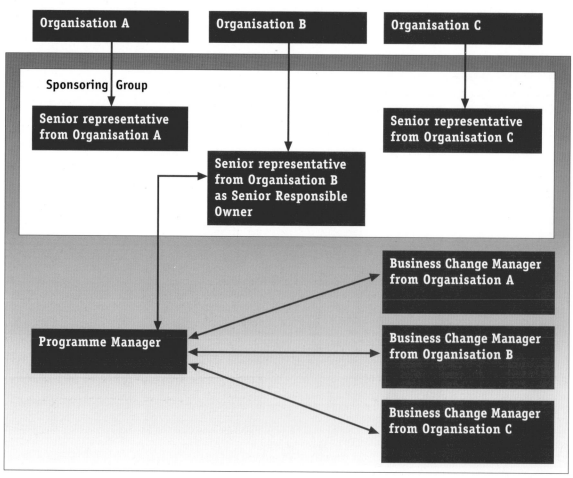

Figure 3.4 Cross-organisational programmes

- **Stakeholder Management**: the need to avoid different and often conflicting messages being passed down the organisations involved in the programme

- **Business Case management**: the organisations involved will invariably have different processes and standards for Business Cases. More flexibility and better control may be achieved if the 'partnership' has a pooled budget

- **risk management and benefits management**: the balance of benefits and risks may vary considerably across the organisations involved. For example, one organisation could carry many of the risks whilst another would expect to achieve the majority of benefits. These imbalances need to be recognised and rewards and incentives applied appropriately.

Some key criteria for cross-organisational programmes are:

- **Goals**: working towards clearly defined, mutually valued, shared goals. If objectives are unclear or not shared, partners may work towards different, incompatible goals and fail to achieve desired outcomes. It is useful to develop a form of contract or memorandum of agreement between the participating organisations to ensure there is a clear and shared understanding. Organisations need incentives to work together because their established practices and procedures can reinforce the primacy of achieving their own objectives rather than joining up. Dealing with cultural differences is often required to enable those involved in joint working to recognise that they may have to compromise and negotiate to ensure the partnership achieves its goals.

- **Progress measurement**: evaluating progress towards achieving the desired goal and taking remedial action when necessary. Cross-organisational programmes are no different from other activities in that their progress must be monitored and remedial

action taken when performance is less than satisfactory. This should include assessing the governance arrangements and revisiting aspects that are proving difficult or problematic.

- **Resources**: ensuring that sufficient and appropriate resources are available. Without sufficient resources, including appropriate skills, a joint working initiative will be difficult to sustain in the longer term, and value for money and propriety may be put at risk. Clear responsibilities and accountabilities need to be defined to ensure appropriate action is taken to resolve resourcing issues.

- **Leadership**: directing the team and the initiative towards the goal. Cross-organisational programmes can be difficult to keep on track because of the additional complexity arising from the number of players involved. Good leadership is an important part of the 'glue' that will hold the initiative together. The role of Senior Responsible Owner is the same for cross-organisational programmes as for any other programme. The additional complexity in cross-organisational programmes is that the individual appointed will be providing leadership and direction to areas and individuals outside their own organisation. All the organisations involved in the programme need to recognise, support and endorse the appointed Senior Responsible Owner.

- **Working well together to achieve a shared responsibility**. If organisations do not establish good working relationships, based on mutual support and trust, acknowledging their differences and sharing information openly, then joint working will fail and benefits will not be realised. This aspect can be particularly significant when the organisations involved have very different cultures and values. It may be useful to consider identifying some special relationships between key individuals from the participating organisations. These relationships can be developed to help support the inter-working.

3.16 Human Resource aspects for programme organisations

The success of any programme will hinge on the availability of the right people at the right time. These people need to be selected or recruited, developed and then posted out again with the active support of the Human Resources (HR) function. HR policies need to be established covering the reporting and management relationships between staff involved on the programme and staff in the rest of the organisation(s). Programmes and projects typically involve a matrix management approach. It is important that line and functional responsibilities are clearly defined and agreed. It is the responsibility of the Senior Responsible Owner and the Programme Manager to make sure this happens in good time.

Programmes are major undertakings, and personnel appointed to them may be involved full-time, meaning they will effectively leave their 'day job'. They may be involved to such an extent that it becomes impractical for their parent division to attend to their career and personnel needs. The programme may have to take account of staff who are separated from their normal organisational structures in this way by including an HR function within the programme organisation.

The resource effort required for some programme roles might be consistently less than full-time contribution, or it might fluctuate dependent on what is happening in the programme. Staff who divide their time between their normal operational business work and work on the programme will need support to ensure their new job mix is achievable yet challenging. Performance appraisals should accommodate and reflect the importance of integrating business operational work with the delivery from programmes. Programmes are an inherent part of change for organisations, and staff should be supported and enabled to contribute to them.

Programme work should not be seen as a job done 'in spare time'.

Resources provided to the programme may be loaned or seconded from operational and functional divisions. Careful consideration of the issues associated with matrix management or resource pools is needed to ensure that staff are able to move between the programme and their 'day jobs'.

Given that programmes can potentially last for several years, the re-entry of staff from the programme back into the business needs careful consideration and planning. Programme and project experience should be highly valued by organisations and should be reflected in the reward and reposting of programme staff who have gained such experience.

3.17 Procurement considerations

Procurement is a common aspect on programmes. It may involve the acquisition of resources or services (or both). Some programmes may involve one or more supplier organisations under formal partnering contracts such as PFI/PPP.

Programme organisations will require access to procurement expertise to carry out or advise on procurement activities, including contract management. Procurement expertise may come from outside the programme, or the programme organisation may include a dedicated procurement function.

There may be pre-existing contractual relationships that provide opportunities for economies of scale or scope for the programme. However, some of these relationships may inhibit the programme in some way. It is important to review existing contractual arrangements across the participating organisations to assess their impact on the programme and develop plans to maximise opportunities and minimise contentions.

4 Benefits management

4.1 Introduction

The fundamental reason for beginning a programme is to realise benefits through change. The change may be to do things differently, to do different things, or to do things that will influence others to change.

Figure 4.1 shows a simple view of the cause and effect of the programme delivering change. The change results in desired outcomes: the things that happen as a result of the changes made. Benefits are the quantification of these outcomes and are used to direct the programme and inform decision-making along the way. Change

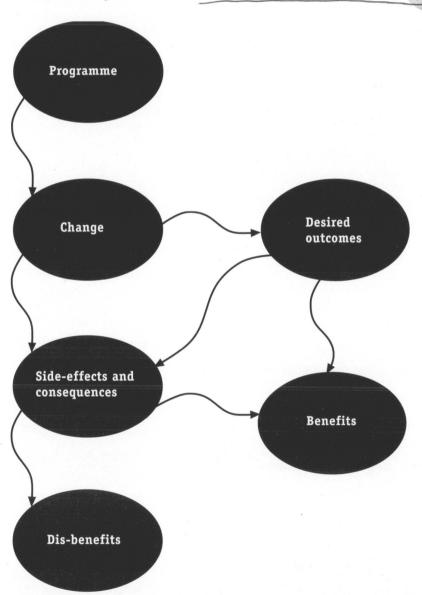

Figure 4.1 Realising benefits through change

may also result in other side-effects and consequences, often leading to 'dis-benefits' – negative impacts of change. Side-effects and consequences may also lead to additional, possibly unplanned, benefits. Benefits management covers all these aspects.

Changes will produce outcomes, but changes alone will not produce measured improvements (benefits). Realising benefits requires active management throughout the change process. The identification, monitoring and measurement of benefits is a fundamental part of successful Programme Management.

The programme's Business Case provides justification for the investment it will require (see Chapter 8). Benefits management works alongside this and enables the programme to plan for and achieve benefits. Costs and benefits cannot be viewed in isolation; the benefits management approach and the overall management of the Business Case are closely connected.

The projects within the programme will deliver new capability; the focus of benefits management is on the realisation of benefits from this new capability. After completion of the programme, the benefits management process will continue because some benefits, possibly the majority of them, may not come on stream until well after the programme has been completed. A degree of post-delivery support by the programme is often required to help business operations take full advantage of the new capability or service delivered.

The objectives of benefits management are to:

- ensure benefits are identified and defined clearly, and linked to strategic outcomes

- ensure business areas are committed to the identified benefits and their realisation, to encourage ownership and responsibility for 'adding value' through the realisation process

- proactively manage the process of benefit realisation, including benefit measurement

- keep benefits within realistic boundaries of scope and value, to identify their wider impact

- use the benefits to direct the programme and provide a focus for delivering change, to realise benefits in line with overall business direction and strategy

- ensure benefits realisation is tracked and recorded, and ensure achievements are properly identified and recognised

- provide alignment and clear links between the programme, its vision and desired outcomes, and the strategic objectives of the organisation(s) involved.

4.2 The benefits management process

Benefits management is a core activity and a continuous 'thread' throughout the programme. It provides the programme with a framework for benefits realisation and a means of monitoring achievement against its targets.

The benefits management process begins with the description of the required outcomes and moves on to developing the programme's framework for the management and realisation of benefits. It involves the following activities (see Figure 4.2):

- developing a Benefits Management Strategy; establishing the structures and functions required; identifying the roles and responsibilities; establishing ownership and management commitment requirements

- identifying, from the desired outcomes, what the benefits are likely to be. Outcomes can also be negative, so dis-benefits should also be considered

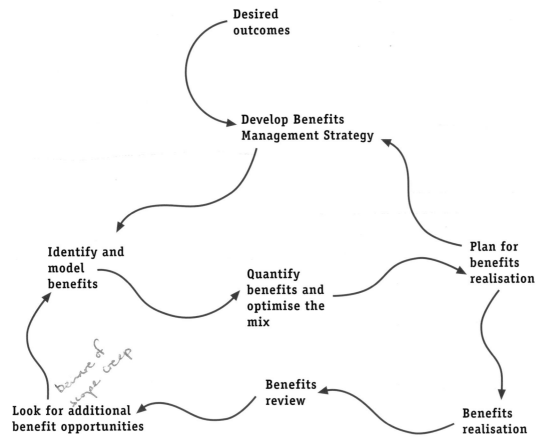

Figure 4.2 The benefits management process

- modelling the benefits (and dis-benefits) to identify any sequences and dependencies

- defining and quantifying the benefits in Benefit Profiles. All benefits must be clearly understood by the business areas responsible for realising them. The commitment and ownership from appropriate senior managers should be established

- planning how the benefits will be realised and measured; understanding the offset of benefits against the costs of realising them; allocating responsibility and ownership

- managing and monitoring the realisation of benefits as systematically as the tracking of costs

- reviewing the realisation of benefits against plan

- assessing the business environment for factors that may influence the realisation of future benefits or affect the improvements from realised benefits

- looking for further leverage from realised benefits; spotting opportunities to realise additional benefits; watching for unexpected benefits or dis-benefits.

Realising the benefits, and making the necessary changes in order to do so, will have an impact (positive or negative) on stakeholders. Close integration between benefits management, stakeholder communications and the other aspects of Programme Planning is required to ensure the programme remains aligned to its target.

4.3 The Benefits Management Strategy

The Benefits Management Strategy is crucial, because it sets out the delivery framework for achieving the programme's strategic objectives (defined in the Vision Statement, Section 7.11). The Benefits Management Strategy should define how benefits will be quantified and measured, what the combined set of benefits looks like, what systems and processes will be used to track progress, and how benefits realisation will be achieved.

The Benefits Management Strategy is an integral part of the programme's strategies and plans. It should reflect and align with the Blueprint to ensure the benefits are matched to the delivery of capabilities.

Table 4.1 Areas where benefits may be identified	
Area where benefits may be identified	**Description**
Policy or legal requirement (mandatory)	Benefits that enable an organisation to fulfil policy objectives, or to satisfy legal requirements where the organisation has no choice but to comply
Quality of service	Benefits to customers, such as quicker response to queries or providing information in a way the customer wants
Internal management	Benefits that are internal to the organisation, such as improving decision-making or management processes
Process improvement (productivity or efficiency)	Benefits that allow an organisation to do the same job with less resource, allowing reduction in cost, or to do more
Personnel or HR management	The benefits of a better motivated workforce may lead to a number of other benefits such as flexibility or increased productivity
Risk reduction	Benefits that enable an organisation to be better prepared for the future by, for example, not closing off courses of action, or by providing new ones
Flexibility	Benefits that allow an organisation to respond to change without incurring additional expenditure
Economy	Benefits that reduce costs whilst maintaining quality (often referred to as cost reduction)
Revenue enhancement or acceleration	Benefits that bring increased revenue, or the same revenue level in a shorter timeframe, or both
Strategic fit	Benefits that contribute to the desired benefits of other initiatives, or make them achievable

Implementation of the Benefits Management Strategy needs to be co-ordinated with all the other programme disciplines, such as risk management, Business Case Management and the management of the Project Portfolio.

A key aspect of benefits management is to ensure that any wider benefits or contributions to benefits have not been overlooked. The Benefits Management Strategy should be regularly reviewed and updated throughout the programme, as a minimum at the end of each tranche. The following sections describe the issues around, and typical content of, the Benefits Management Strategy. For further details on the content of a Benefits management strategy, see Appendix B.

4.3.1 Checking the Benefits Management Strategy

When the Benefits Management Strategy has been developed, the following checks can be helpful to ensure it is complete:

- does the total set of benefits match the required outcomes from the programme?

- have the relevant stakeholders been sufficiently engaged with the development of the strategy?

- does the organisation have the necessary capabilities and capacity to deliver the strategy?

- have appropriate accountabilities and responsibilities been identified and allocated?

- is the strategy integrated with the other plans and strategies related to the programme?

4.4 Identifying benefits

The desired outcomes will be articulated in the organisation's business strategy or policy development process. The outcomes should be clearly defined as part of the Programme Mandate (see Chapter 8). The outcomes provide the basis for identifying the programme's benefits, which are the quantification of improvements described by the outcomes.

Benefits may be identified in a number of different areas, as shown in Table 4.1.

4.4.1 Outcome relationship modelling

In some situations, the detailed understanding of potential outcomes cannot be completed before the programme gets started, in which case the programme team should work with the strategy or policy teams to develop the required level of detail. One approach for doing this is to build a model of the outcomes and consider how these interrelate and affect the environment in which they will operate (see Figure 4.3).

Figure 4.3 shows a cause and effect model of outcomes and their relationships in the area of education. The outcomes are shown in ellipses and the arrows indicate a relationship to other outcomes. The example shows that 'improved teacher motivation' will lead to 'improved teacher retention'. It may be difficult to quantify and value (that is, measure) improved 'motivation'. However, the example shows 'motivation' is linked to 'retention', so by identifying benefits in 'retention' levels (measuring the improvements), the programme can infer the achievement of 'improved motivation'. The example also highlights that creating 'more teachers' will not be achieved simply because there is 'improved teacher retention'. There will need to be other initiatives in place to actively increase the number of teachers, such as improvements in teacher recruitment schemes. Having established the overall model of outcomes, the benefits that will provide the direction and focus for the programme can be identified.

4.4.2 Dis-benefits

In many situations, not all outcomes will be positive. There will often be some 'dis-benefits' (negative benefits) from the programme. Dis-benefits should be identified, measured and tracked in the same way as benefits. Management effort will be required to seek to

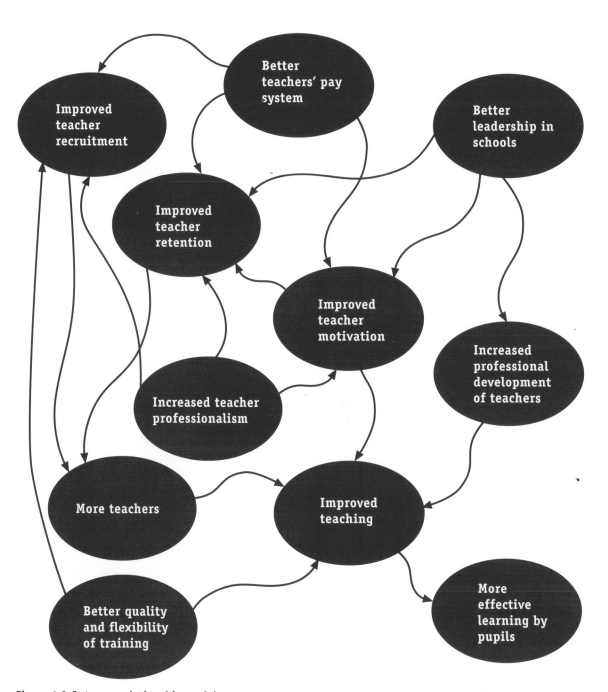

Figure 4.3 Outcome relationship model

minimise the impact of dis-benefits on the overall improvements from the programme.

Some dis-benefits may not be easy to identify at the start of a programme, but will surface later on. For example, the provision of a central booking service for

parking facilities may have the dis-benefit that the parking attendants will no longer have local knowledge of parking availability that customers find useful.

There may be inherent dis-benefits that no amount of planning or forethought can eliminate completely. An example might be the introduction of a new system that transfers decision-making from the central office to individual business units. Greater flexibility and responsiveness to the customer benefit the organisation as a whole, but for individual units, the obligation to take on more tasks is a dis-benefit. Also, at an organisational level, there might be a loss of control and different standards of service as business units might begin to diverge.

4.4.3 Benefit ownership

Each benefit should be 'owned' by an appropriate senior manager to ensure accountability for successful delivery. Ownership of the overall set of benefits rests with the Senior Responsible Owner. One way to make this 'ownership' meaningful is to link benefits realisation to personal performance targets.

4.5 Quantifying benefits

Ideally, benefits should be quantified and measured in monetary terms. However, this is not always possible and may not be the best approach for measuring achievement. Even if monetary quantification is not possible, all benefits should be quantified numerically. For example, the emergency services might perceive a reduction in the time to treat a victim as a desired outcome, in which case the benefits would be related to measures of time. Another example might be the social services wanting to reduce the number of children 'at risk'. There may be costs associated with maintaining the 'at risk' register, which could be measured, but the key measure would be the number of children actually 'at risk'.

There is often a tendency to be over-optimistic when defining and quantifying the expected benefits from a programme. Unfortunately, over-optimistic expectations can inhibit the buy-in and commitment from staff and cause the benefit reviews (see Section 4.9) to become 'witch hunts'.

4.5.1 Benefit categories

There are several different types of benefit:

- direct financial benefits: those that are realised by the programme and can be measured in monetary terms, for example, x% increase in revenue

- direct non-financial benefits: those that are realised by the programme but are difficult or impossible to measure in monetary terms

- indirect benefits: those that result either from the direct benefits or from other changes made by the programme. For example, benefits may accrue to other organisation(s), groups or individuals who cannot be directly engaged with the programme itself but are influenced by it.

Many change programmes aim for outcomes such as changing the culture of the organisation, or improving the working environment. These benefits are often referred to as intangible or 'soft' benefits. Valuing these intangible benefits will require careful consideration of the measures that will indicate whether they have been realised.

Care should be taken to avoid defining benefits that cannot be measured. If a benefit cannot be assessed in any realistic way it is usually better not to claim it at all.

4.6 Benefit Profiles

The benefits (and any dis-benefits) need to be defined in detail so that the programme can monitor and track their progress. The full description of a benefit is called the Benefit Profile and includes details of the measures, ownership responsibilities, links and dependencies, costs associated with realisation and measurement, and the period of time over which the benefit will be realised.

For further details on the Benefit Profile see Appendix B.

4.7 Benefit modelling

Benefits (and dis-benefits) do not typically happen in isolation. The realisation of some benefits will depend on activities and projects, organisational changes, or on the realisation of other benefits. These dependencies will play an important part in the prioritisation of programme activities, so it is important to recognise and identify them.

It may be helpful to create a benefits model, covering the entire set of benefits and showing how they

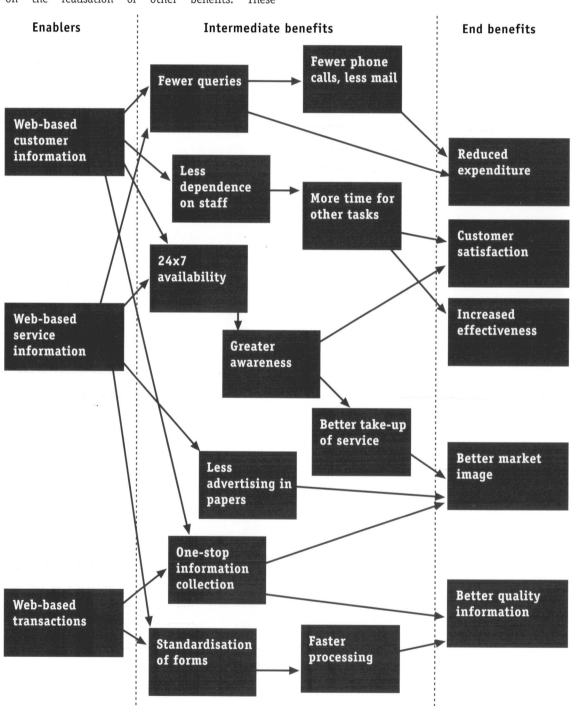

Figure 4.4 Example benefits model

interrelate, both with each other and with the projects in the programme's portfolio. Using the Benefit Profiles, consider what each benefit's prerequisites are and how it fits into the total 'picture' of changes. The benefits model should include any assumptions or requirements that are outside the scope or control of the programme that may affect the planned realisation of benefits.

Some benefits will take longer to deliver measurable improvements than others. It is useful to consider shorter-term benefits as well as the longer-term ones to ensure there is sufficient ongoing focus and commitment to the programme. Shorter-term benefits are more likely to be realised, and demonstrate clearly to all stakeholders that the programme is a successful one. Benefits that are not going to be realised for many years, perhaps not until long after the programme has closed, may generate less commitment and enthusiasm. Using the benefit model, the focus on longer-term benefits can be improved by identifying those interim activities or benefits that will directly contribute to the longer-term ones. Figure 4.4 shows an example benefit model with the benefits and their inter-relationships.

4.8 The Benefits Realisation Plan

Delivery and realisation of the benefits will take place at the business operations level. The programme will deliver the new capability, service, or working practices, and will enable the business operations to implement these. Realising the measurable effects of the change means embedding the new capability into the business operations so that it becomes part of 'business as usual'. Realisation of the full set of benefits may not happen until after the final project in the programme has completed (see Figure 4.5).

The Benefits Realisation Plan is a complete view of all the Benefit Profiles in the form of a schedule defining when each benefit or group of benefits will be realised and any handover activities that are required. The Benefits Realisation Plan will be developed alongside the Programme Plan (see Chapter 7) and the Business Case (see Chapter 8) to ensure close alignment between delivery of capability and realisation of benefits against the associated costs and risks. It may be helpful to consider merging the Benefits Realisation Plan and the Programme Plan.

The 'people' aspects associated with change should not be underestimated. Good preparation and adequate lead times are required to enable those involved in the change to accommodate and accept new ways of working, new systems, new environments, etc. This may include people outside the organisation. Successful realisation of benefits relies on the total commitment and involvement of those affected within an organisation, as well as understanding from those outside it. The development of the Benefits Realisation Plan should be closely integrated with the programme's strategies for Stakeholder Management and communications.

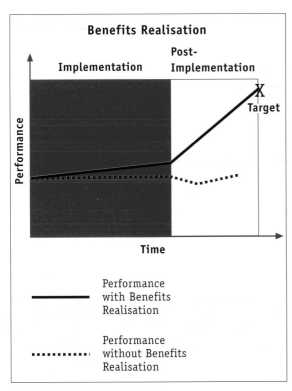

Figure 4.5 Benefits realisation

The Benefits Realisation Plan will identify appropriate points for carrying out benefit reviews to formally assess the realisation of benefits.

For details of the content of a Benefits Realisation Plan see Appendix B.

4.9 Reviewing benefit realisation

Programmes are typically significant and highly visible to the organisations involved, the organisations they affect, and to those that are affected by the outcomes, both inside and outside these organisations. Throughout the programme, it is important to monitor how far the benefits remain valid and valuable in the eyes of stakeholders.

Input from stakeholders, including the business managers responsible for the changed operations, will provide realistic information and evidence of benefits realised. To avoid conflicts of interest, the realisation of benefits should not be assessed by those directly involved.

The objectives of benefit reviews are:

• to assess and update the Benefit Profiles and Benefits Realisation Plan to ensure that the planned benefits remain achievable and have not changed in scope or value

• to check that the overall set of benefits remains

Table 4.2 Responsibilities for benefits management	
Benefits management process	**Responsibilities**
Developing the Benefits Management Strategy	Developed on behalf of the Senior Responsible Owner by the Programme Manager and Business Change Manager(s) representing the affected business areas, and relevant stakeholders. The Senior Responsible Owner 'owns' the Strategy
Identifying and quantifying benefits	Business Change Manager(s) representing the affected business areas, relevant stakeholders, the Programme Manager and members of the project delivery teams. Input and approval from the Senior Responsible Owner and members of the strategic planning teams as required. The Business Change Manager(s) 'own' the Benefit Profiles
Planning for benefits realisation	Business Change Manager(s) representing the affected business areas, relevant stakeholders, the Programme Manager and members of the project delivery teams. Approval from the Senior Responsible Owner and members of the strategic planning teams as required. The Programme Manager 'owns' the Benefits Realisation Plan
Benefits realisation	The Business Change Manager(s) as part of their line management role in business operations. Programme Office for monitoring progress against plan
Benefit reviews	The Senior Responsible Owner is responsible for leading the reviews involving relevant stakeholders, business managers, and possibly internal audit. The Programme Office is responsible for ensuring the information gathered from the reviews and the assessment of benefits is disseminated appropriately

aligned to the programme's objectives, and to reprioritise or realign them as necessary

- to inform stakeholders and senior management of progress in benefits realisation, and to help identify any further potential for benefits

- to assess the performance of the changed business operations against their original (baseline) performance levels

- to assess the level of benefits achieved against the planned Benefits Profiles

- to review the effectiveness of the way benefits management is being handled, so that improved methods can be developed and lessons learned for the future; for example, improving the definition of benefits, or improving the understanding of the organisation's capability to deliver.

4.10 Responsibilities for benefits management

The Senior Responsible Owner is ultimately accountable for the overall realisation of benefits from the programme. However, benefits management will involve responsibilities across the entire Programme Management Team and many of the programme's stakeholders. Table 4.2 indicates who is involved throughout the benefits management process.

5 Stakeholder Management and communications

5.1 Introduction

Over the life of a programme, there will be many individuals or groups with an interest or involvement with it, or who are affected by its activities and outcomes. These are the programme's stakeholders. They include those managing and working within the programme and those who are directly or indirectly contributing to, or affected by, the programme or its outcomes (see Figure 5.1).

Whether stakeholders are individuals or groups, it is vital to remember that they are all human beings, with feelings, perceptions, desires and influence. In any change situation, there will be those who support the change and those who oppose it. There will be those who gain from it and those who lose – and those who are convinced they will lose despite all evidence to the contrary. There will be those who anticipate an opportunity and those who see only a threat. There will, of course, be those who are indifferent to the change; this may turn out to be helpful or unhelpful, depending on the influence they have. Understanding stakeholders' interests in the programme, and the impact that the programme will have on them, and then implementing a strategy to address their issues and needs, is an essential part of successful Programme Management.

5.2 Identifying stakeholders

Stakeholder Management begins with identifying all the stakeholders involved in or affected by the programme. The programme's Vision Statement and Blueprint provide the basis for identifying who the stakeholders are and what outcomes they want.

During the lifetime of the programme, stakeholders may come and go, depending on the activities of the programme. Key stakeholders, such as the programme's sponsors, should (hopefully!) remain constant

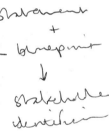

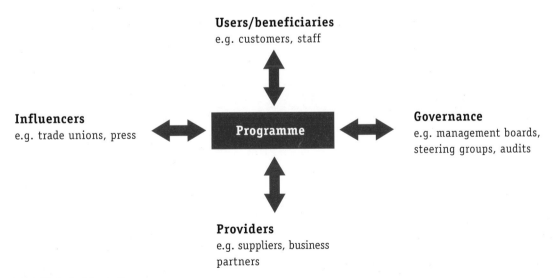

Users/beneficiaries
e.g. customers, staff

Influencers
e.g. trade unions, press

Programme

Governance
e.g. management boards, steering groups, audits

Providers
e.g. suppliers, business partners

Figure 5.1 Stakeholder influences

throughout the programme. Some stakeholders will be able to participate in the programme in advisory or assurance roles; others will be important in assessing the realisation of the programme's benefits; others will have an audit perspective.

Stakeholders may be identified from the following groups (see also Figure 5.2):

- owners or shareholders, executive management, operational management and staff of the organisation(s) who are:

  - sponsoring the programme

  - affected by the programme

  - supplying goods or services to the programme or its constituent projects

  - supplying goods or services to organisation(s) affected by the programme

- customers or consumers who will be affected by the programme's outcome

- internal and/or external audit

- security

- Trade Unions

- political or regulatory bodies

- the wider community in which the affected organisation(s) exists, such as the general public

- project management teams delivering the projects within the programme

- the Programme Management Team, including the Sponsoring Group.

The list of stakeholders could be long, possibly extremely long. It may be helpful to list stakeholders under categories such as 'governance', 'influencers', 'users/beneficiaries', 'providers' (see Figure 5.1). Each category can then be broken down further if necessary.

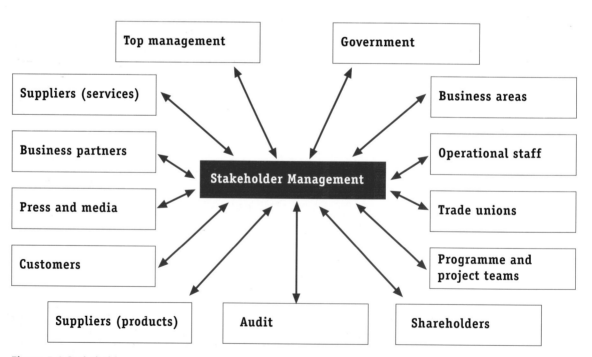

Figure 5.2 Stakeholders

Categories should be recognisable groups rather than abstract categories, for example, 'employees based in one geographical location' is a readily identifiable group, whereas 'members of the public who support human rights' is not. Some categories may identify the same individuals, but it is often useful to differentiate between stakeholders 'wearing different hats'.

5.2.1 Stakeholder Map

Stakeholders will inevitably have different interest areas in the programme, for example, some will be concerned with how the programme will affect their working environment; others will want to influence how the programme will change the way customers are handled. A Stakeholder Map (see Figure 5.3) is a useful way of mapping the various stakeholders against their interests in the programme and its activities and outcomes.

5.3 Stakeholder Management Strategy

An important component of any programme is the Stakeholder Management Strategy, which describes **who** the stakeholders are and **what** their interests and influences are likely to be, **how** the programme will engage with them, **what** information will be communicated and **how** feedback will be processed by the programme.

Implementing the Stakeholder Management Strategy means considering a range of factors including:

- the scale of cultural, organisational or societal change

- management of expectations over an extended period

- the need for business ownership of the overall programme

- the need for staff buy-in and involvement

- the need for marketing and communications expertise to support the programme

- the requirement for clarity and consistency of messages and benefits.

Failure to address any one of these areas can affect the successful outcome of the programme.

The following sections describe how to develop the information required for a Stakeholder Management Strategy. For further information about the contents of a Stakeholder Management Strategy see Appendix B.

Interest area

Stakeholders	Strategic direction	Financial	Operational changes	Interface with customers	Public safety	Competitive position
Business partner	●	●		●		●
Project teams			●			
Customers		●		●	●	
Press and media						●
Trade unions			●			
Staff	●		●			
Regulatory bodies		●			●	

Figure 5.3 Example Stakeholder Map

5.4 Analysing stakeholders

The objective of analysing stakeholders is to achieve a thorough understanding of their requirements and their interest in, and impact on, the programme so that communications address their particular interests, issues and needs. Stakeholders' positions (in terms of influence and impact) may be rational and justifiable, or emotional and unfounded, but they must all be taken into account since, by definition, stakeholders can affect the change process and hence the programme.

Because there are typically large numbers of stakeholders with widely varying degrees of interest and influence, it is useful to analyse the significance and potential power of each individual stakeholder or stakeholder group. This analysis will also provide a basis for the prioritisation of Stakeholder Management communications, which will help the programme concentrate resources where they will contribute the most towards a successful outcome.

It also helps to ensure that communication channels are targeted appropriately and that messages, media and levels of detail reflect the needs of the relevant stakeholders. The communications channels may need to accommodate stakeholders who cannot be engaged directly with the programme. In many cases, working through partners, industry groups, volunteer organisations, etc. may be required.

One technique for analysing stakeholders is to consider each stakeholder in terms of their importance to the programme and the potential impact of the programme on them and 'plot' them on a matrix (see Figure 5.4). The level of their importance to the programme and potential of its impact on them will determine the level and type of Stakeholder Management activities the programme should adopt. For example, an investment partner will have a 'high' status of importance to the programme, and, depending on the scale and opportunities for any return on their investment, the impact of the programme on them may be 'low', 'medium' or 'high'.

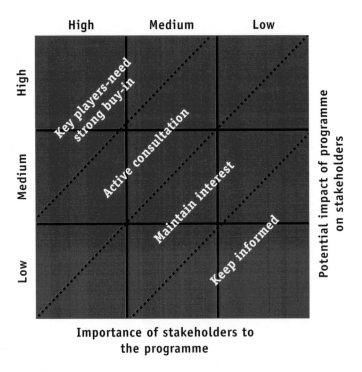

Figure 5.4 Power/impact matrix

Stakeholders may move up or down the matrix as the programme progresses, so it is important to revisit the stakeholder analysis work during the programme. Responsible stakeholders can and should enhance and even alter the course of the programme.

5.5 Stakeholder communication

Communication is central to any change process. The greater the change, the greater the need for clear communication about the reasons and rationale behind it, the benefits expected, the plans for its implementation and its proposed effects.

The objectives of the communications process are to:

- keep awareness and commitment high

- maintain consistent messages within and outside the programme

- ensure that expectations do not drift out of line with what will be delivered.

Successful communications will be judged on the ability to meet these objectives.

Successful communications are based on four core elements:

- message clarity: to ensure relevance and recognition

- stakeholder identification and analysis: to send the right message to the right audience

- a system of collection: to obtain feedback and assess the effectiveness of the communications process

- a system of delivery: to bring the above together.

Messages must be consistent. They should be few in number, simple, and brief, and derived from the programme's objectives. It may be useful to use touchstone statements, soundbites or wordbites as the foundation for more complex communications and then to repeat these throughout the programme. This approach will help stakeholders to recognise specialised elements within an understandable framework. It also ensures the organisation is seen to be speaking with one voice.

5.6 The Communications Plan

The Communications Plan describes **what** will be communicated and the authority required, **how** it will be communicated, by **when**, and by **whom**, during the programme. It should be defined and implemented as early as possible and then maintained throughout the programme.

Using information from stakeholder analysis, the Communications Plan should be designed with the following objectives:

- raising awareness amongst all stakeholders of the benefits and impact of the Blueprint

- gaining commitment from staff in the target business area(s) to the changes being introduced – thus ensuring the long-term success of the improvements

- keeping all staff in the target business area(s) informed of progress before, during and after implementation or delivery of project outcomes

- promoting key messages from the programme

- demonstrating a commitment to meeting the requirements of those sponsoring the programme (the Sponsoring Group)

- making communications truly two-way by actively encouraging stakeholders to provide feedback and ensuring they are informed about the use of their feedback to influence the programme. All types of feedback should be expected, and responses to it carefully considered. Feedback may sometimes be negative, impractical or harshly critical

- ensuring all those responsible for projects have a common understanding of the changes involved in the programme

- maximising the benefits obtained from the new business operations.

A key objective is to communicate early successes (sometimes referred to as 'quick wins'), both to those directly concerned with the business operation and to other key audiences, especially where rapid progress in realising benefits is required. The aim is to secure commitment and build momentum. Thereafter, effective communications will facilitate knowledge transfer across programme staff and into the business operations.

The Communications Plan should answer the following questions:

- what are the objectives of each communication?

- what are the key messages?

- who are the stakeholders the communications are trying to reach?

- what information will be communicated and by whom?

- when will information be disseminated, and what are the relevant timings?

- how much information will be provided, and to what level of detail?

- what mechanisms will be used to disseminate information?

- how will feedback be encouraged, what will be done as a result of feedback?

The answers to these questions may be different for each of the stakeholder groups. The Stakeholder Map, developed during analysis, can be extended to list the specific communications activities for each stakeholder group.

For further information about the Communications Plan see Appendix B.

5.7 Communication channels

Communication channels should be established to ensure that stakeholders' expectations of the programme can be managed and maintained throughout the programme's life. An ongoing two-way interface between the programme and its stakeholders is essential.

The channels used for communications may be a mixture of 'participative' approaches, for example, seminars or workshops, and 'non-participative' media, for example, announcements or newsletters. The effectiveness of each channel used should be monitored as the programme progresses. Changes should be made to cater for the evolving requirements of the stakeholders, as their knowledge increases and demand for information grows. Some possible channel options are summarised in Table 5.1.

5.8 Managing stakeholders

To support the programme's formal communication processes, there will always be the need for more subtle and informal means of communication. The Programme Management Team will often need to influence, lobby, cajole, manipulate, co-opt, flatter and apply pressure to stakeholders in order to maintain momentum and keep the programme on track.

The following checklist will help focus on ensuring the overall approach to managing the programme's stakeholders is robust:

- is there a common and shared understanding of what is meant by 'stakeholder'?

Table 5.1 Communication channels

Channel	Purpose and benefits
Seminars and workshops	Powerful tools for communication to specific groups of stakeholders. A key benefit is that they provide the Programme Management Team with an opportunity for direct contact with stakeholders and for obtaining first-hand feedback on issues directly affecting them
Press/media	The press and media are vehicles for getting messages about the programme to an external audience and for providing the Programme Management Team with confirmation that their work is significant and important
Bulletins, briefings, announcements, press releases (web- or paper-based)	There are two types: (1) general information about the programme for all audiences, and (2) specific information relevant to one or more stakeholder groups General information should provide an update on the programme, addressing issues of concern to all stakeholders, such as overall progress or any changes to the programme objectives The more specific information should provide the particular stakeholder(s) with information relating to their own issues Distribution may be via Intranet home pages, websites or email. However, it is important to make sure that stakeholders have access to email or the web pages, are aware of their existence, and want to visit them. In addition to electronic, it is often useful and more convenient to distribute in paper form, such as newsletters Frequently asked questions (FAQs), together with appropriate responses, are often included
Site exhibitions	Static displays are useful in providing a continuing 'presence' and awareness within the organisation about the programme
Video and CD	Video films, when targeted appropriately, are a cost-effective means of communication to large, widely dispersed audiences and can be used to provide updates on progress and for 'selling' the key programme messages CDs are useful for presenting large amounts of information about the programme by enabling individuals to search for information relevant to their particular interests

- is there a detailed set of stakeholder groups and are they being targeted in practice?

- are targets or goals set for each group or set of groups?

- is there a clear Communications Plan for achieving these targets or goals?

- are the relevant members of the Programme Management Team strongly motivated to achieve these targets or goals?

- do key stakeholder groups feel sufficiently engaged in the programme, and do they understand the programme's objectives and constraints?

- is feedback from stakeholders measured and acted upon?

5.9 Responsibilities for Stakeholder Management

The Programme Manager is responsible for the development and implementation of the Stakeholder Management Strategy and Communications Plan. However, other members of the Programme Management Team will typically be involved in the consultation with stakeholders. For example, the influencing of key stakeholders may fall to the Senior Responsible Owner.

Programmes involving changes to working practices will need the support and commitment of those who will be operating them. Generating the confidence and buy-in of those involved is the responsibility of the Business Change Manager(s).

The Programme Office is responsible for maintaining the information relating to stakeholders and facilitating the activities defined in the Communications Plan.

6 Risk management and issue resolution

6.1 Introduction

Programmes are established to deliver change through the co-ordinated execution of multiple projects. Programmes typically involve diverse groups of stakeholders, together with contributions from service providers, suppliers and other third-party organisations. This, together with the inevitable upheaval caused by change, makes the programme environment uncertain, complex and dynamic. At any point during a programme, there will be events or situations that may adversely affect the direction of the programme, the delivery of its outputs, realisation of expected benefits or the achievement of desired outcomes. These events or situations are the risks and issues that the programme has to manage and resolve.

Risks are things that may happen at some point in the future and require positive management to reduce their likelihood of happening, their impact on the programme, or both. Issues are things happening now that are affecting the programme in some way and need to be actively dealt with and resolved. Risks, should they occur, become issues.

The task of risk management is to keep the programme's exposure to risk at an acceptable level. It is never possible to remove all risks. Some risks may actually present positive opportunities to improve some aspect of the programme, and recognising any such opportunities should be part of considering what action to take should a particular risk occur.

Issues can arise at any time during the programme, and will require specific and usually immediate management action. Issues at the project level will typically be handled by the project's problem/incident reporting mechanisms, only being escalated to the programme level should the project be unable to resolve them. The task of issue resolution is to prevent the issue from threatening the programme's chances of achieving a successful outcome.

Both risk management and issue resolution should be formally incorporated in project level standards for the projects operating within a programme. These standards should also include 'rules of engagement' between the projects and the programme level. Projects will need to have mechanisms for escalating issues or risks to the programme and for participating in the resolution and management activities associated with these issues and risks. Risks and issues cannot always be contained at the project level. For example, there may be a one-off issue facing a particular project, which if left unresolved, could effectively undermine the entire programme. These 'killer' issues will need to be escalated and resolved at the programme level.

6.2 Risk management overview

Effective leadership and management of a programme means constantly monitoring the risk situation and implementing appropriate and timely action based on informed analysis of the risks. The purpose of risk management is to inform decision-making and enable realistic and practical judgements to be made on what actions to take. The causes of risk arise in many areas, including the environment of the programme, the change process itself, changes to the vision, changes to the scope or content of the programme or its projects.

Risk management involves having processes in place to monitor risks; having access to reliable and up-to-date information about risks; using the appropriate controls and actions to deal with risks; and having appropriate decision-making processes – all defined within an overall Risk Management Framework.

Figure 6.1 shows the basic elements of risk management, which are described in the following sections.

More detailed guidance on the management of risk can be found in OGC's *Management of Risk: Guidance for Practitioners*.

6.3 The Risk Management Strategy

The programme's framework for risk management is defined and documented in the Risk Management Strategy. The Risk Management Strategy sets the context in which risks will be identified, analysed, controlled, monitored and reviewed. It is important that the approach to managing risk is consistent with the broader 'appetite' for risk within the organisation's culture and general work practices. For example, organisations that are normally risk-averse in their approach

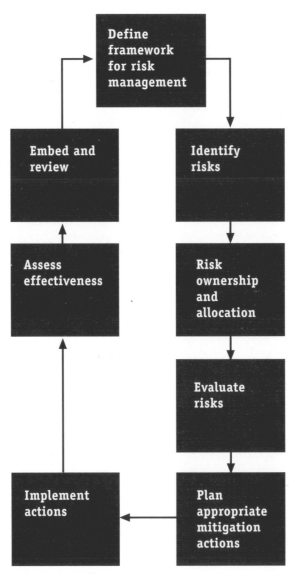

Figure 6.1 Risk management

to business are unlikely to succeed with high-risk programmes, because the level of risk will be more than the organisation is prepared for or able to cope with.

The Risk Management Strategy should address each of the elements shown in Figure 6.1, which are discussed in the following sections. For more information on the Risk Management Strategy see Appendix B.

6.4 Risk identification

Identifying risks to the programme will be a continuous activity throughout the programme's life. Identifying risks means considering what exactly is at risk – timescales, resources, delivery of new capability or realisation of benefits, for example. It is unlikely that all possible risks will be identified; as a guideline, a realistic expectation should be to identify the 20% of risks that would have 80% of the potential impact.

Risks should be documented in the programme's Risk Register, which is the central repository of information about the risks and provides the basis for prioritisation, action, control and reporting. The Risk Register will contain a large volume of information, and it is useful to present an overall picture of the programme's risk profile showing how many risks fall into the high-probability, high-impact area. These major risks will require senior management attention to monitor appropriate actions and continually assess the overall profile.

Risks can include the concerns of senior management as well as more 'tangible' potential problems, which are often easier to spot. Taking actions to deal with risks can only be done effectively if all risks are included in the Risk Register.

The Risk Register will be continually updated and reviewed throughout the programme. For details of what a Risk Register should contain see Appendix B. Appendix C may be a helpful starting point for considering where risks might come from.

6.4.1 Strategic level risks

Considered risk-taking can enable organisations to take an innovative approach to seeking greater opportunities for realising benefits. At this level, there are drivers (such as political pressures, emerging technologies and new initiatives) arising while the programme is underway, which may alter the programme's scope and lead to changes in direction – a source of further risk to the programme.

The failure to achieve a common understanding among members of the Sponsoring Group and other stakeholders about the programme's objectives is a risk in itself. Not having a common understanding means not only that success is unlikely, but that it is not possible to tell whether 'success' has been achieved. Such failure will, of course, affect the direction and chances of success of the entire programme.

There are also likely to be risks around programme interdependencies that need to be considered as these programmes are scoped and planned. Changes at the strategic level, such as new initiatives that the organisation must respond to quickly, can affect programme interdependencies and the associated risks.

6.4.2 Programme-level risks

A major area of risk to the programme is where project interdependencies change, giving rise to new sources of risk. The realisation of the programme's benefits may be frustrated if such risks are not managed.

Other risks to the programme may arise if the underlying assumptions of the programme's Business Case change, potentially making the Business Case invalid (due to market changes or competition, for example). It is helpful to include explicit statements of any assumptions made in order to flag up potential risks of this nature.

6.4.3 Project-level risks

Much of the focus of the management of risk within programmes is at the project level. Some project risks may be identified before the projects are underway, for example when the programme is being set up. When project teams analyse risks, they may gain clearer insight into risks affecting the programme, necessitating a revision of the programme's risks. Further risks may be identified due to non-availability of skills and resources that will affect the project's capability to deliver its products or services. Project-level risk management must be integrated into the risk management processes at the programme level – typically with the support of the Programme Office.

6.4.4 Operational level risks

As projects deliver their outputs of products and services, the transition to new ways of working and new systems can lead to further sources of risk. For example, during a handover process, risks could arise from the need to maintain 'business as usual' as well as the integrity of the systems, infrastructure and support services.

6.5 Risk ownership and allocation

Risk management is primarily the responsibility of the Programme Manager. However, each identified risk should be allocated to an individual who is best placed (with relevant seniority, authority and responsibility) to monitor it and manage any appropriate mitigation or contingency actions. In many instances, this ownership will fall to the Programme Manager, but the Senior Responsible Owner and other members of the Sponsoring Group are equally likely to be identified as the most appropriate risk owner.

On major or complex programmes, the responsibility for risk management may be assigned to a dedicated Risk Manager role. The individual appointed to this role will work with the Programme Manager and will have specialist expertise in managing risks.

6.6 Risk evaluation

Evaluating each risk involves assessing the probability of its occurring and the potential impact should it occur. Risks are not all equal in either their probability or their impact. Some risks may have the potential to halt the programme should they occur. It may be useful to set tolerance levels for as many risks as possible to assist with prioritisation of management actions. For example, the risk of staff shortages could be set with a tolerance level of 80% of full complement.

Actions should be defined such that, if the risk approaches its tolerance level, the risk owner reports the situation to the programme (usually the Programme Manager) and is able to take appropriate action.

6.7 Responses to risk

Each risk will have a range of possible mitigation actions that will affect either the probability of the risk occurring or its impact should the risk occur; these can be summarised as 'the four Ts':

- **transfer** the risk to the third party best placed to manage it, for example by taking out an insurance policy. Some risks, such as reputational risk, cannot be transferred

- **tolerate** the risk – basically the 'do nothing' option, which means the programme will use existing management arrangements to handle the results of the risk happening. Typically used for 'low-impact' risks. Sometimes, this response can be just as risky as a more proactive response, particularly in an environment of constant change

- **terminate** the risk by adjusting the programme so that the risk no longer applies, for example, by removing those activities that would lead to a particular risk

- **treat** the risk by identifying and implementing

mitigating actions that address either the probability or impact of the risk and so contain it at an acceptable level.

6.8 Implementing actions

Having determined the most suitable responses to the identified risks, the relevant actions should be planned, resourced and implemented. Risks and the selected responses to them should be communicated to stakeholders, particularly those who are directly affected either by the risk itself or by the actions taken to contain the risk.

6.9 Assurance and effectiveness of risk management

The programme's arrangements for, and implementation of, risk management should be assessed at appropriate points during the programme, as a minimum at the end of each tranche.

Not all identified actions aimed at reducing the probability or impact of the risk will be successful. The assessment of the risk management processes should include how effective any mitigation actions have been and whether the risk identification activities identified the risks that have in fact materialised.

The presentation of information about the programme's risks and the associated management actions should be carefully considered in terms of the audience. For example, top-level reviews of the programme's overall risk profile could present the most significant risks in the form of a matrix (impact against probability) with a simple 'traffic light' system to focus attention on the critical risks. More detailed reviews will require lower levels of detail, including specific progress on agreed mitigating actions.

Some critical success factors for the effective management of risk are:

- nominated individuals with clearly defined responsibilities to support, own and lead on risk management

- a pragmatic risk management approach, and the benefits of following it, clearly communicated to all personnel involved with the programme

- an organisational culture that supports well thought-through risk-taking

- management of risk fully embedded in management processes and consistently applied

- management of risk closely linked to achievement of programme objectives and benefit delivery

- risks actively monitored and regularly reviewed on a constructive, 'no blame' basis.

6.10 Embedding risk management

Risk management takes time and is not an optional programme task. It needs to be an intrinsic part of the way the programme is planned and run. It is also important to ensure the Risk Management Strategy is kept up to date by reviewing and amending it to reflect practical experience. The Risk Management Strategy and Risk Register should be accessible to everyone with an interest in the programme.

6.11 Issue resolution

In a similar way to the formality necessary for managing risks, resolving issues also requires the programme to determine how issues will be handled and resolved efficiently. The purpose of issue resolution is to build a mechanism for the programme to deal efficiently with anything that arises by having processes and responsibilities in place. It is impossible to anticipate everything that could possibly happen during the programme, so planning how to deal with the unknown, and usually unplanned, is important.

6.12 The Issue Resolution Strategy

The Issue Resolution Strategy sets out how issues will be captured and assessed prior to the appropriate resolution activities being carried out. It should cover the activities and considerations shown in Figure 6.2. Information is necessary for effective assessment of the

potential impact of an issue. The Issue Resolution Strategy defines how the relevant information for assessment will be collected, who will be responsible for resolution activities, and how ownership of the issues raised will be allocated.

Assessing issues typically classifies them into one of the following three types:

- a previously identified risk which has now happened and requires the appropriate risk management action

- a required change to some aspect of the programme

- a problem or question affecting all or part of the programme in some way.

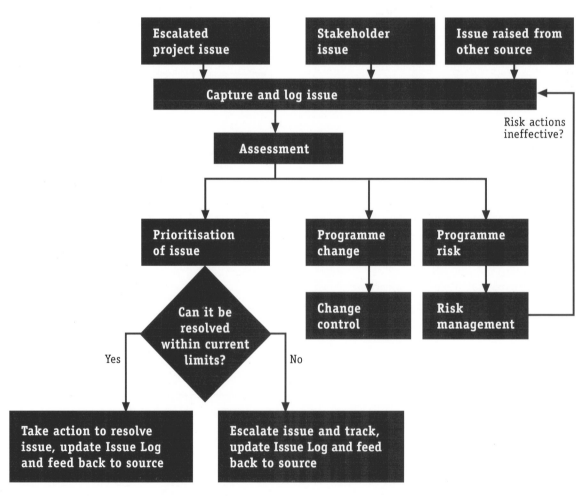

Figure 6.2 Issue resolution process

Prioritisation of issues is a key part of issue resolution. The volume of issues facing programmes can be huge. It may be helpful to develop prioritisation criteria to provide a filter to focus on critical issues.

For further details on the Issue Resolution Strategy see Appendix B.

6.13 Sources of issues

Issues are likely to arise from a wide variety of sources, for example:

- benefits management, transition activities, costs, scope, timescales

- dependencies, quality of operations, resources, programme deliverables

- anything that the project level cannot resolve, or issues common to more than one project

- stakeholders, organisation and programme staff, third parties

- other projects and programmes underway within the organisation.

All issues raised, from whichever source, should be captured and logged on the programme's Issue Log. The Issue Log provides a management tool for the Programme Manager in the ongoing tracking and monitoring of issue resolution.

6.14 Resolving issues

Issues may suggest some kind of change to the programme. The options for change should be considered and actioned appropriately as part of the programme's change control process (see Section 6.16).

When identified, issues may in fact turn out to be possible future events rather than present concerns. Such issues should be moved to the Risk Register and managed under the Risk Management Framework.

Issues that are not dealt with through change control or risk management should be prioritised in terms of their actual or probable impact on the programme. Some issues, for example, queries from stakeholders or requests for information, should be responded to as quickly as possible. Other issues may not be resolvable within the limits of the current resources, timeframe, or scope of the programme. These issues should be escalated to the appropriate top management level for resolution.

The status and resolution of issues should be included in the Issue Log for audit trail and future reference. For further details on the Issue Log see Appendix B.

6.15 Cross-programme issues

Some issues may, individually, have an impact across many parts of a programme or across more than one programme. The resolution of these issues should still be handled within the programme's formal issue resolution process. However, the priority given to these issues will inevitably be high because of the need to consider the wider implications of any management action or intervention.

Cross-programme issues may involve any aspect of the programme, for example, internal or external resources, suppliers, stakeholders, changes to requirements or escalation in costs. As with all issues, they should be captured and formally assessed in terms of their impact (whether actual or potential) on the programme. Typically, cross-programme issues need to be escalated to top management for resolution. It is important to establish and maintain effective communication channels between top management and the appropriate members of the Programme Management Team, particularly during the resolution of cross-programme issues (see Chapter 5).

6.16 Change control

A critical aspect of resolving issues is the process of making changes to the programme. Change control is the process of managing and controlling changes to any aspect of the programme, the projects, or the project outputs. In a programme context, change control should be applied to the key sets of information about the programme, such as the Blueprint, the Business Case and the Programme Plan. The process may also be applied to products during their development stages on a project. In this case, change control would be applied at the project level. Change control should be closely integrated with the programme's Configuration Management activities (see Chapter 9).

Defining the procedures for change control on a programme requires consideration of the following:

- maintaining a central log of potential changes – the Issue Log

- establishing a mechanism for prioritising the potential changes

- carrying out formal impact assessments of the potential changes against the programme's Business Case, Programme Plan, Project Portfolio, Blueprint, etc.

- assessing the impact of the change on the risks to the programme, or the expected benefits

- re-evaluating the priority status

- decision processes for deciding which changes to accommodate

- updating the Issue Log with the decision and maintaining an audit trail

- implementing the approved changes appropriately and communicating the outcome to those affected.

6.17 Integration between the programme and its projects

All project-level issues and risks must also be visible at the programme level, since individual projects may not be able to perceive their wider implications to other projects or the programme itself. Ultimately, responsibility for all the risks and issues within the projects lies with the programme (specifically with the Programme Manager), but they will differ in terms of who is best placed to manage and resolve them.

Each project team within the Project Portfolio is responsible for its own change control procedures. However, certain changes will have an impact outside the project, either on other projects within the Project Portfolio or on the Programme Plan. The programme should specify the tolerance levels for any such changes at the project level so that only those changes that matter to the programme are escalated to the programme level. It is important for all the project teams to have a common understanding of the change control process for the programme. The aim is to balance the need to communicate changes to all interested parties with the overhead of too much administration.

The Programme Office should play a central role in building and maintaining efficient two-way flows of information between the programme and its projects. The Programme Office should 'own' the processes of risk management and issue resolution for the programme.

6.18 Responsibilities for risk management and issue resolution

The Programme Manager is responsible for the development and implementation of the strategies for handling risk and issues. Managing specific risks is the responsibility of those best placed to carry out the necessary response actions or mitigation plans. Similarly, the resolving of issues is done by those with the relevant authority and responsibility.

The Senior Responsible Owner is responsible for ensuring the risk management and issue resolution activities are operating effectively, and that key strategic risks and issues facing the programme are dealt with at the appropriate senior level.

The Programme Office is responsible for managing and co-ordinating the information and support systems to enable the programme's risks and issues to be handled efficiently.

7 Programme planning and control

7.1 Introduction

Programme planning and control is not simply project planning and control on a larger scale, rather it is a combination of various planning and monitoring considerations. All these aspects have a part to play and are set out and brought together in the Programme Plan, a key control document for the programme. The relationship between the elements of Programme Planning, and the central Programme Plan, is shown in Figure 7.1.

7.1.1 The Vision Statement

The programme's Vision Statement provides one of the early inputs to Programme Planning by setting out the outcome(s) that the programme is aiming to achieve. The Vision Statement is an outward-facing description of the new capabilities resulting from programme delivery. The new capability might be to deliver a particular service, to perform the same service but in a more efficient way, or simply to be better than the competition. The Vision Statement will describe the new services, improved service levels, or innovative ways of working with customers, or any combination.

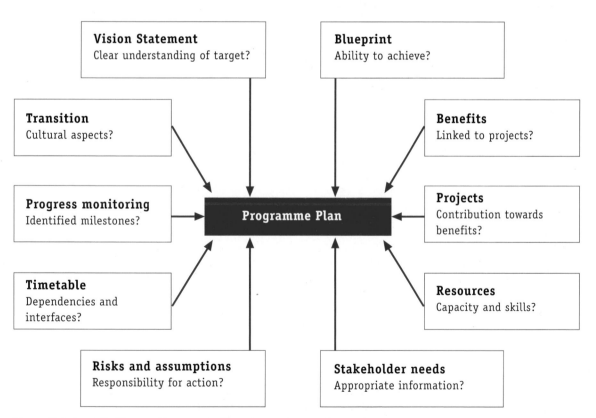

Figure 7.1 Contributions to Programme Planning and control

For further details on the Vision Statement see Appendix B.

7.1.2 The Blueprint

The Blueprint is a model of the business or organisation, its working practices and processes, the information it requires and the technology that will be needed to deliver the capability described in the Vision Statement. It describes the people, processes, information and technology capability in the new or future 'state' that will be capable of realising the benefits expected and achieving the outcomes desired. For further details on the Blueprint, see Appendix B.

7.1.3 Benefits

The programme's benefits will be realised following successful business change (see Chapter 4). The total set of Benefit Profiles, together with the Benefits Realisation Plan, needs to be integrated with the development of the Programme Plan to ensure the dependencies on project delivery are considered.

7.1.4 Projects

The Project Portfolio is a list of all the projects and activities that together will deliver the required future state described in the Blueprint and allow the organisation to acquire the capabilities described in the Vision Statement. It includes information on existing projects, new projects that will be commissioned by the programme, and any related workstream activity required to support the projects or enable them to start. The Project Portfolio will include work that will be in place at programme startup as well as work that will be initiated during the programme.

7.1.5 Resources

Any input required by a project is known as a 'resource'. The term covers people, assets, materials, funding and services. Shared resources should be planned and managed at the programme level. Developing the Programme Plan will identify those resources that need to be shared between projects. Minimising resource sharing between projects will help prevent bottlenecks,

while maximising it will help promote knowledge sharing, organisational learning and joined-up working.

7.1.6 Stakeholders

The Programme Plan contains a key set of management information about the programme. Building and sustaining relationships with stakeholders requires two-way communications about the programme and its progress (see Chapter 5).

7.1.7 Risks

Implementing the Programme Plan will inevitably have risks associated with it. Assumptions will be made about the programme and its progress; the projects may face critical risks that, if they should happen, will affect the entire programme. The identification of these, together with suitable mitigation actions, should be part of the programme's risk management activities and included in the programme's schedule. For further details on risk management see Chapter 6.

7.1.8 Timetable

The drivers for the programme may include given and immovable deadlines over which the programme has little or no control, such as the launch date for a new currency. These time-related drivers will naturally restrict the overall timescales within which the programme must operate. The Programme Plan should integrate the timetable for project delivery and transition with the timetable for benefits realisation (the Benefits Realisation Plan).

7.1.9 Progress monitoring

During the implementation of the Programme Plan, the Programme Management Team will need to establish the continual monitoring of progress. The end of each tranche of the programme represents the key review points (or milestones) at which a formal assessment of progress and benefits realisation can be made. These reviews may involve internal assurance, peer-level assessors, audit, or external scrutiny, depending on the type of programme and its governance requirements. For further details on reviews see Chapter 9.

As the programme progresses, the Programme Plan and its related information are reviewed and updated. Progress against the Programme Plan is monitored to ensure the programme remains on track to deliver the desired outcome(s). Throughout this monitoring process, management interventions will be necessary to address problem areas and prevent the programme drifting off target.

7.1.10 Transition

Change to an organisation or business, its people, working practices, information and technology needs to be planned and managed carefully to allow for the cultural and infrastructural migration from the 'old' environment to the 'new' one. Transition management is a crucial part of Programme Planning. It begins as the projects approach completion and continues until the new business operations are self-supporting and fully embedded. Maintaining 'business as usual' is an important consideration during transition, since new operations will be introduced while the existing ones are still operating.

7.2 Planning and scheduling

Programme planning is a continual activity throughout a programme. At the beginning of a programme, it involves determining and defining **what** needs to be done and **when**, **how long** things should take, **who** will do them, **how** will things be monitored, **who** needs to be involved, and **what** risks may affect progress. This information is captured in the Programme Plan.

The key steps in the planning process include:

- the formulation and design of the Project Portfolio

- the construction of a schedule of project delivery

that demonstrates realisation of benefits aligned with the strategic objectives that set the context for the programme

- the integration of the increasing refinement of individual project plans as each project proceeds through its stages into the Programme Plan to inform and assess progress

- responding to exception situations on the projects (either external influences or internal variances) that will cause a reappraisal and review of the Programme Plan

- continual monitoring and review of progress against the Programme Plan, including anticipating any emerging risks to the Programme Plan.

Developing and maintaining the Programme Plan requires the ongoing co-ordination of all the project plans. The focus for Programme Planning is on the interdependencies between the projects and any dependencies on external factors outside the control of the programme. The projects involved in the programme will inevitably experience the day-to-day problems associated with keeping on track. Delays in one area will affect other areas, thus making Programme Planning and monitoring a complex task.

7.2.1 Programme scheduling

The Project Portfolio describes the projects required by the programme. Each of the projects will have a project plan indicating the time required to complete it, and information about its interdependencies with other projects within the programme.

A dependency network model is useful to show the inputs and outputs of projects and how they contribute to or depend on others. Treating each project as a 'black box' enables the Programme Manager to schedule projects according to their dependencies, and to assess the impact of any potential slippages. Figure 7.2 shows an example dependency network.

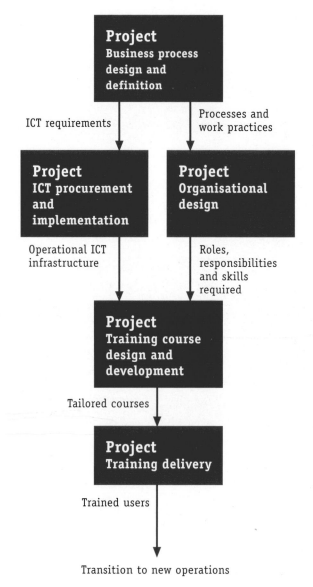

Figure 7.2 Example dependency network

The programme's schedule provides the overall sequence and timetable for the programme by incorporating the dependency network and the timescales for each of the projects. The schedule can be used to determine critical paths and pressure points during the programme where management attention should be focused.

7.2.2 Tranches

The schedule and Benefits Realisation Plan (see Chapter 4) should help to identify those points during the programme at which sufficient projects will have been completed to enable a review of early benefits and to assess the overall progress of the programme. The programme schedule should be divided into 'tranches' (groups of projects) reflecting these step changes in capability and benefit realisation. The end-point of each tranche falls at the end of the project within it that finishes last. Tranches can overlap, and some may run for such a period that other tranches begin and close while they are still in progress.

Figure 7.3 shows an example programme schedule indicating the grouping of projects into tranches and the review points.

7.2.3 Prioritisation

Prioritisation is a key factor influencing programme scheduling. The effect on staff and the rest of the programme of delaying or bringing forward a particular project can be significant. Prioritisation should focus on the critical programme activities, for example:

- specific projects, such as procurements whose outputs are prerequisites for future projects

- resource requirements, such as specific skills that may be scarce

- early benefit realisation, such as reduced operational costs that will help engender continued commitment and enthusiasm for the programme.

7.3 Managing resources

A major part of Programme Planning is to consider what resources the programme will require, and how they will be used and managed effectively. Programme resources will include:

- the programme's finances, budgets, expenditure profiles and accounting procedures

- the staff and other personnel involved in the programme, including those who will be affected by its outcome(s)

- the assets the programme will use; buildings and equipment, for example

- the systems, services and technology the programme will use and develop as part of delivery.

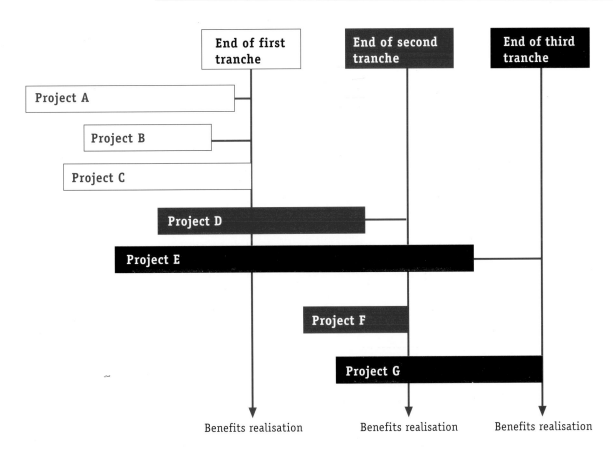

Figure 7.3 Example programme schedule

The Resource Management Strategy should identify the resources required, how they will be acquired, how they will be managed, and in particular, how resource sharing will be handled.

Typical examples of resource sharing are:

- staff – where people are involved with more than one project within the programme

- infrastructure or facilities – for example, where office space may need to be shared

- information – for example, where a group of projects may be updating a shared repository

- third-party services – where several projects make use of the same service provider.

Shared resources represent a set of dependencies between projects and therefore need to be used efficiently.

The Resource Management Strategy should be developed alongside the Programme Plan to ensure the resources required match the planned activities and timescales.

For further details of the Resource Management Strategy see Appendix B.

7.4 Programme-level control

Managing the programme does not mean micro-management of the projects within it. Providing information that affects the projects, and ensuring the right information from the projects is passed up to the programme level, is a major consideration when establishing programme-level controls.

The aim of the programme is to realise the expected benefits and to achieve the desired outcomes; the aim of the projects is to deliver the required outputs. This difference may lead to tensions between the project- and programme-level planning and control processes.

One of the greatest challenges in running a programme is therefore to reconcile project objectives and accountability with overall programme goals and programme-level consistency and control. Factors such as project management experience, programme risk and available tolerance should all be assessed when determining how tightly the programme controls its projects.

The communication flow between the programme and its projects should aim to reuse information that is part of the management standards implemented across the Project Portfolio. Project documentation such as Project Initiation Documents (PIDs), highlight reports, exception reports, Issue Logs and Risk Registers will provide much of the information required by the programme. It is important to establish common project-level reporting standards across the Project Portfolio to minimise any reworking of information for the programme level.

7.4.1 Project control

The degree of control that the programme level should exercise over individual projects will vary depending on the nature of the programme. The most effective way to ensure delivery of a single project is to assign accountability, responsibility and authority for its success to the project management team. However, absolute delegation runs the risk of projects making decisions that further their own objectives, whilst perhaps compromising the overall vision or design integrity established by the programme. Conversely, directing all aspects of control centrally is a costly exercise, complicated by the breadth of specialist knowledge needed at the centre to manage what is by definition a multidisciplinary endeavour.

Each project should have its own direction-setting and decision-making processes, with individuals responsible for leading and managing these processes. Project-level governance should be formally integrated with programme-level governance to ensure the projects remain aligned to the objectives of the programme. The programme level should focus on project interdependencies and the risks and issues that may affect the programme as a whole.

7.4.2 Integration of information

The main areas to consider for integration of programme- and project-level information are:

- strategic level changes that alter the programme's Blueprint, Vision Statement or Business Case and will have an impact on 'live' projects, or those soon to start

- responsibilities and ownership of any risks and issues that are managed at the programme level but may have an impact at the project level

- tolerance levels for project-level costs, timescales and quality

- project-level milestones and review points.

7.5 Progress monitoring and performance measurement

Programmes are typically made up of numerous distinct projects and activities, which between them produce a wide range of outputs. Monitoring progress of the programme towards its target outcome(s) requires proactive identification and measurement of those elements (processes, activities or outputs) that significantly affect the projects and activities in terms of total process efficiency, effectiveness, quality, timeliness, productivity or safety.

The Programme Plan is a 'living entity', providing the definitive up-to-date snapshot of the programme. It provides the basis for monitoring and tracking the impact of each project on the programme's overall objectives, benefits, risks and costs, and making adjustments as necessary. It also enables the Programme

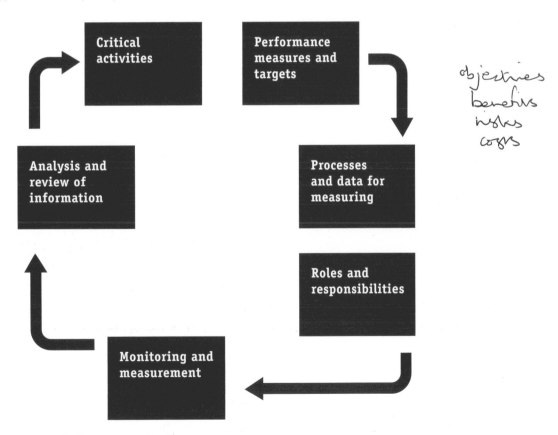

Figure 7.4 Progress monitoring framework

Manager to monitor the dynamics of the inter-relationships between projects, and to act when a delay in any one project might jeopardise the work of others. For example, if benefits in one area are no longer achievable due to external changes, this will have a ripple effect across the whole programme.

Figure 7.4 shows the activities involved in defining and implementing a framework for monitoring progress.

The Programme Plan should identify those projects or activities that are critical to the programme's progress. These should have specific performance measures and targets identified that will indicate whether progress is on track or not. Targets are quantified objectives that express the aims of the process, activity or output being measured. They should be realistic but challenging. Good targets will be SMART: Specific, Measurable, Achievable, Relevant and Timed. They should give a balanced overall picture of the programme. Unbalanced targets and performance measures, with gaps or biases in coverage, may result in perverse incentives or promote undesirable behaviour. For example, measuring the quantity of letters answered but not the usefulness of the responses may not encourage a better quality service.

The processes, data capture and resources put into collecting and analysing data for monitoring and measuring purposes should be proportional to the benefit that the resulting information brings. The amount of time and effort required to monitor progress should be balanced with that applied to the measurement of achievement of the desired outcomes and benefits realised. Both monitoring progress and measuring performance are important aspects of Programme Planning and control. The Benefit Profiles and the Benefits Realisation Plan identify the relevant performance measures for each benefit as well as how and when performance will be assessed. The Programme Plan should integrate this information with the necessary monitoring and performance assessment of the programme as a whole.

There is a variety of techniques that can be used for monitoring progress. For example, the concepts of 'earned value' can be applied to some programmes where the actual work completed can be represented in terms of its financial worth and proportion of the total 'value' of the programme.

There are also various approaches for measuring performance. Some useful performance measurement techniques are given in Appendix D.

7.6 The Programme Plan

The Programme Plan is not a 'master' project plan, it is a key control document for the programme that forms a complete picture of how the programme is going to work. It enables the Programme Manager, on behalf of the Senior Responsible Owner, to implement a planned and controlled environment that can be monitored and maintained throughout the life of the programme.

The Programme Plan should include:

- project timescales, costs, outputs and dependencies

- risks and assumptions

- schedule showing the programme's tranches

- transition plan

- monitoring and control activities and performance targets.

For further details of the contents of a Programme Plan see Appendix B.

Developing the Programme Plan requires an understanding of the following:

- what level of detail the Programme Plan should go to in order to provide adequate information about progress and to provide a usable management tool for identifying 'pressure points' and other issues that may affect progress

- what tools will be used to monitor and maintain the Programme Plan, including how information from the Programme Plan will be presented to stakeholders, and how project-level information will be integrated at the programme level

- what information from the Programme Plan will be distributed, to whom, and when, as part of achieving the required communications for the programme (see Chapter 5).

7.7 Responsibilities for Programme Planning and control

The Senior Responsible Owner is responsible for approving the Programme Plan and leading the monitoring activities, including the reviews at the end of each tranche. The reviews should measure the performance of the programme in terms of the benefits realised and outcomes achieved (see Chapter 4).

The Programme Manager is responsible for designing and implementing the Programme Plan, the Resource Management Strategy and the required monitoring and control activities. The Programme Manager will need to

work closely with the Business Change Manager(s) to ensure that the Programme Plan, Benefits Realisation Plan and Benefit Profiles are consistent and maintained in line with progress.

The Business Change Manager(s) is responsible for managing the transition and will need to work closely with the Programme Manager on designing the Project Portfolio and scheduling the projects to ensure the transition will align with the required benefits realisation.

The Programme Office is responsible for supporting the Programme Manager in the development and implementation of the planning and control activities. It is also responsible for collecting monitoring and measurement data, keeping the information up to date and publicising it regularly so that affected and interested parties are kept fully informed and able to provide feedback as appropriate.

Another responsibility of the Programme Office is ensuring there are coherent and common project-level standards in place and for all document management arrangements for the programme. It will provide the same service to the projects within the Project Portfolio.

Specific
Measurable
Achievable
Relevant
Timed

8 Business Case management

8.1 Introduction

The Business Case is an aggregation of specific information about the programme: benefits and the risks to achieving them, costs and timescales. The Business Case presents the optimum 'mix' of this information that can be used to judge whether or not the programme is (and remains) desirable, viable and achievable. The Business Case effectively describes what the *value* is to the sponsoring organisation from the outcomes of the programme. Managing the Business Case is about *value management* of benefits, costs, timescales and risks.

There will be a Business Case for the programme as well as separate (but linked) project-level Business Cases. At the project level, the Business Case is about balancing the costs, timescales and risks relating to the specific outputs of the project. The programme-level Business Case embraces the wider horizons of strategic outcomes from the programme's projects. The programme-level Business Case provides the summation of the project-level Business Cases to present the programme's overall balance of benefits and costs against strategic objectives. The Business Cases at both programme and project levels are constantly monitored, reviewed regularly (as a minimum at the end of each tranche), and updated as necessary to provide the stimulus for ensuring that progress remains aligned to the strategic objectives (see Figure 8.1).

The following sections discuss the development and content of the programme's Business Case.

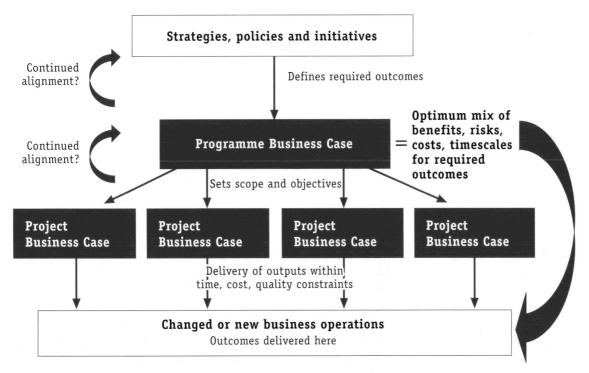

Figure 8.1 Programme and project Business Cases

8.2 The evolution of the Business Case

8.2.1 Drivers for the programme

Before a programme can begin, the organisation's senior executives and top management team will need to define and agree the policies or business strategies for the organisation. This will involve considering high-level options for how these strategies might be delivered, and prioritisation of new and existing work against these strategies.

Successful delivery can only be achieved by a realistic assessment of organisational capability and capacity in terms of delivering the strategies. Being ambitious is challenging, but achieving success requires a realistic view of the organisation's capability, capacity and culture to accommodate change.

8.2.2 The Programme Mandate

A Programme Mandate triggers programme startup. The Programme Mandate articulates the strategic objectives for the programme, optimum strategies for delivery, the improvements that are expected to result, and how the programme fits with other initiatives. This information sets the scene for a controlled startup for the programme. It informs and directs the activities of programme identification and definition.

For further details on what the Programme Mandate should contain see Appendix B.

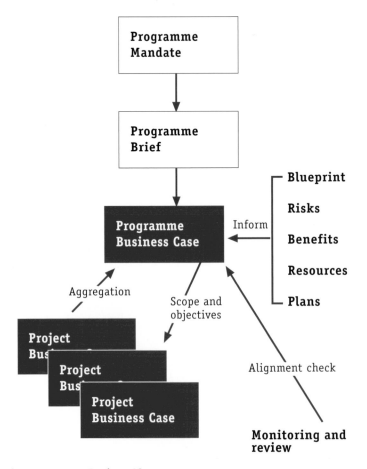

Figure 8.2 Developing the programme Business Case

8.3 The Business Case

The programme's Business Case sets out the overall costs, the anticipated benefit realisation, and the risk profile of the programme, in order to assess its viability and make appropriate management decisions about its continued viability. It is unlikely to be developed in its entirety, in a single pass, at the very start of setting up a programme. Its content will be developed from the Programme Brief (itself developed from the Programme Mandate) and refined as more information becomes available.

The Business Case is developed by iteration through these early stages of formulation and analysis, and is completed with information from other Programme Management functions, including benefits management, risk management, financial planning and scheduling (see Figure 8.2). The Business Case is an aggregation of information developed in other programme documentation and from project level information.

There are usually options to consider in terms of how the programme's outcome could be achieved. The options will require detailed consideration to be able to compare the likely costs, benefits, and risks associated with each option.

Throughout the programme, the integrity of information included in the Business Case and the related documentation should be maintained and kept up to date – thus providing an auditable trail between the Business Case and the progress of the programme.

The Business Case presents the substantiated picture of the complete programme right through to delivery and realisation. It provides the programme's leadership and sponsors with an objective decision-making tool to ensure the programme is on track and remains on track.

The Business Case and the Blueprint (see Chapter 7) will be developed in parallel and will require close integration to ensure the benefits to be delivered are driving the programme's transformation. Developing the Business Case alongside the Blueprint enables the programme to select the most cost-effective combination of projects and activity workstreams.

The design of the programme's Blueprint should be focused on realising the expected benefits within justifiable costs. The Business Case is where a trade-off is made between the costs associated with delivering new capability and realising a benefit, and the value to the organisation(s) of having that benefit. This concept of 'net benefits' is represented by the net benefit line in Figure 8.3. The costs of delivery and realisation may outweigh the value to the organisation(s) during the early stages of a programme. As more benefits are realised, thus providing greater value, so the 'net benefit' increases.

The Business Case is developed during Programme Definition (see Chapter 12). For further information on the content of a Business Case see Appendix B.

8.4 Reviewing the Business Case

The programme's Business Case is reviewed regularly throughout the programme to ensure the programme remains on track. As a minimum, the Business Case

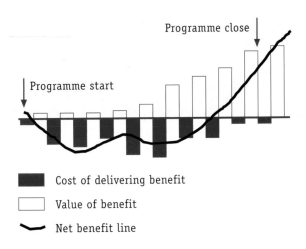

Figure 8.3 Net benefits

should be reviewed at the end of each tranche to assess the need for realignment and the continued viability of the programme.

Reviewing the Business Case should provide answers to the following questions:

- is the programme (still) affordable – is there sufficient funding?

- is the outcome (still) achievable – is there a realistic assessment of the organisation's ability to cope with the scale of change envisaged?

- does the programme (still) demonstrate value for money – are the benefits and the costs of realising them in the right balance?

- have options been considered – is the programme's portfolio (still) the appropriate, or optimum, way of achieving the desired outcome(s)?

8.5 Managing the Business Case

Information presented in the Business Case will serve many purposes during the life of the programme – all focused on ensuring successful delivery and strategic alignment. The Business Case can be used as part of a *value management* approach where the overall 'mix' of benefits, risks, costs and timescales is reviewed and validated against such factors as issues, constraints, and other blockers. Value management is a useful technique for keeping the programme on track to achieve its objectives.

The level of detail and completeness (or maturity) of the Business Case will reflect the amount of uncertainty associated with the programme. Initially, the Business Case information will undoubtedly be uncertain; estimates will be very approximate, with high levels of

potential variance. As the programme develops and more fixed information is known, so the Business Case will become more accurate and complete.

The Business Case provides a single point of reference for justifying the proposed investment. As the programme progresses, it provides the baseline for monitoring the continued viability of the programme. The programme's environment is likely to be dynamic and the influences on the programme itself may cause priorities to alter, or the overall direction of the programme to change. The Business Case will need to be adapted to reflect these sorts of changes and to ensure the programme remains aligned to the strategic direction.

The justification of the programme's investment will be based on the requirement for realisation of benefits to the stakeholders sponsoring the programme. The Business Case contains information on the expected benefits and desired outcomes, and it therefore provides the basis for assessing whether those benefits have been realised and outcomes achieved. Assessment of benefit realisation will happen during the programme (for 'early wins'), at programme closure, or afterwards – depending on what criteria have been set for programme closure (see Chapter 16).

Managing the Business Case will not end until the programme is able to demonstrate delivery of the Blueprint and realisation of the benefits (see Chapters 4 and 16).

8.6 Responsibilities for Business Case management

The Senior Responsible Owner is ultimately accountable to the Sponsoring Group for the successful delivery of the programme and will therefore 'own' the Business Case throughout the life of the programme.

The Senior Responsible Owner is responsible for ensuring the Business Case is monitored, reviewed regularly, and updated with more detailed information as the programme develops and progresses. This involves scanning the business horizons surrounding the programme and will often lead to realignment of the programme in some way. They must also ensure that the progress of the programme remains aligned to the Business Case.

Programmes involving more than one sponsoring organisation may not be able to identify easily the individual who is best placed to 'own' the Business Case. One approach to resolving this issue is to consider the financial input to the programme. Since the financial commitment typically underpins the viability of the programme, the organisation with the largest financial commitment may be best placed for 'ownership' of the Business Case and for providing the individual to fill the Senior Responsible Owner role.

The development of the Business Case and the input of specific information will inevitably require expertise from other members of the Programme Management Team and, in some cases, input from external specialists. The Programme Office will also be involved in collecting and maintaining Business Case information.

The Programme Manager is responsible for updating the Business Case and managing the programme's expenditure against the overall investment defined in it. The programme's Financial Plan contains the detail required to ensure expenditure is adequately controlled. On larger programmes, it may be necessary to appoint a Financial Controller or Programme Accountant to carry out this responsibility on behalf of the Programme Manager.

The Business Change Manager(s) is also responsible for the management of benefits defined in the Business Case. Other responsibilities include detailed definition of the benefits and their measurement at the start of the programme, then tracking them through the programme's portfolio through to realisation.

9 Quality management

9.1 Introduction

Quality, as applied to a programme, embraces many different aspects, including:

- the quality of the programme's leadership and management processes, including the information needed to make decisions and the reliability of the information provided

- the quality of its deliverables, meaning their 'fitness for purpose'

- the quality of its assessment and measurement activities.

Quality management is a continuous process throughout the life of a programme. Achieving quality should be an integral part of the day-to-day activities on the programme. One fundamental aspect of quality is defining quality-checking criteria. There is a wide range of programme activities where quality management is involved:

- Configuration Management and change control of programme documentation, such as the Blueprint and Business Case, to ensure programme status information is up to date and accurate

- quality assurance and review of outputs from the projects to ensure they are 'fit for purpose', meet stakeholder requirements, and can enable the organisation to realise the required benefits and achieve the capability described in the Vision Statement

- quality management of the programme's governance arrangements, including:

  - the roles and responsibilities of the Programme Management Team

- adherence to organisational and industry standards

- the consultation and engagement of stakeholders

- appropriate design and implementation of good practices in Programme Management and delivery.

The following sections describe these aspects of quality in more detail. The Quality Management Strategy should cover management processes and procedures for all these activities.

9.2 Configuration Management

No organisation can be fully efficient or effective unless it manages its assets well, particularly if those assets are vital to the running of the organisation's business.

Configuration Management is a well-established discipline applied widely on projects and in product development, particularly within manufacturing and engineering. It is the process of ensuring that all individual components or sub-products of a complete product (the configuration) are identified and maintained, that changes to them are controlled, and that releases into operational use are done on the basis of formal approvals. When dealing with the components involved in manufacturing a car, for example, Configuration Management ensures that the right component is fitted in the right place to the right model of car. The application of Configuration Management within a Programme Management environment is no less significant.

The purpose of Configuration Management is to identify, track and protect the programme's assets or products. In a programme context, the products that are of material interest will include the following:

- the Vision Statement – the statement of the desired outcome(s) linked to the organisation's strategic objectives

- the Blueprint – the definition of all aspects of the organisation that has the capabilities expressed in the Vision Statement

- the Benefits Realisation Plan – detailing when the benefits are expected to be realised. The realisation of benefits is inherently linked to the achievement of the desired outcome(s)

- the outputs from the projects – defined in the Project Portfolio, with links to the benefits to which the outputs are contributing. The outputs are therefore linked to the benefits, which are in turn linked to the outcome(s).

The configuration of the programme's products needs to be internally consistent and represent a coherent picture of the overall programme. Without Configuration Management, a programme can be severely disrupted with, for example, trying to reconcile project deliveries with out-of-date benefits expectations.

The inevitable changes that arise during a programme will have an impact on one or more of the programme's products. Configuration Management requires the effective control of change. For further details on change control see Chapter 6.

9.2.1 Configuration Items

The assets or products of a programme are known as Configuration Items (CIs). There will be a variety of products of interest to the programme; the following categories may help to identify them.

- Programme CIs such as Vision Statement, Blueprint, Business Case, Programme Plan and Benefits Realisation Plan. Each of these represents a particular aspect of what the programme is about. Together they form a complete picture of the programme's objectives, how these objectives will be met, what benefits are expected, at what cost, and when they will be realised.

- External CIs such as the organisation's business strategy or other policies that are internal to the organisation but independent of the programme. Regulatory or statutory requirements also form external products that the programme needs to track, as do products shared between more than one programme. These will help determine the scope of the programme and may also present constraints on the programme.

- Internal CIs, comprising those delivered by individual projects, including tangible outputs such as buildings, and 'softer' results such as new competencies in staff.

Each CI needs to be uniquely identified, whether it is generated inside or outside the programme. The identification should also differentiate between successive versions.

Each CI should have one or more discrete states through which it can progress. The significance of each state should be defined in terms of what use can be made of the CI. There will typically be a range of states relevant to the individual CIs. However, the minimum coverage could be:

- draft – denoting that the CI is 'under development' and that no particular reliance should be placed upon it

- approved – meaning that the CI may be used as a basis for further work

- withdrawn – meaning withdrawn from use, either because the CI is no longer fit for purpose or because there is no further use for it.

The way CIs will move from one state to another should be defined. This will include defining the type of review and approval required and the authority level necessary to give that approval.

9.2.2 Baselines

The set of approved CIs will form a 'baseline' configuration. Each baseline is a mutually consistent set of CIs that can be declared at key programme milestones. The programme may progress through a series of baselines, each providing successively further levels of detail towards the eventual outputs and outcome(s) required. Figure 9.1 shows an example of how a number of baselines may be built up for the programme.

Each baseline forms a frame of reference for the programme as a whole, or possibly a separate one for each of its tranches. Baselines provide the basis for assessing progress and undertaking further work that is internally self-consistent and stable. For example, the Vision Statement, Blueprint, Programme Plan, and Business Case should present a consistent and clear definition of what the programme is intending to do. This may form the 'scope baseline' (see Figure 9.1) for the programme and give internal and external parties a clear basis for subsequent analysis and development.

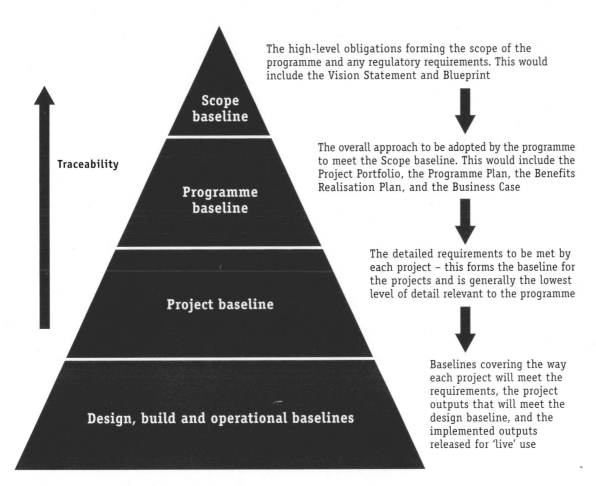

The high-level obligations forming the scope of the programme and any regulatory requirements. This would include the Vision Statement and Blueprint

The overall approach to be adopted by the programme to meet the Scope baseline. This would include the Project Portfolio, the Programme Plan, the Benefits Realisation Plan, and the Business Case

The detailed requirements to be met by each project – this forms the baseline for the projects and is generally the lowest level of detail relevant to the programme

Baselines covering the way each project will meet the requirements, the project outputs that will meet the design baseline, and the implemented outputs released for 'live' use

Scope baseline

Programme baseline

Project baseline

Design, build and operational baselines

Traceability

Figure 9.1 Configuration Management baselines

Each baseline provides progressively greater levels of detail regarding the eventual outputs to be delivered. Furthermore, this hierarchy of baselines enables the final outputs to be traced back to the original requirements.

There are five basic activities involved in Configuration Management:

- **planning**: deciding what level of Configuration Management is required for the programme and planning how this level will be achieved

- **identification**: identifying and uniquely naming all the assets or products of interest to the programme

- **control**: establishing and operating the mechanisms for identifying when individual products or complete configurations will be agreed and 'frozen' ('baselined') so that future changes are only made with appropriate levels of agreement and approval

- **reporting**: recording and reporting of all current and historical information concerned with each product and configuration

- **reviewing**: a series of reviews or audits to ensure there is conformity between the documented baselines and the actual business environment to which they refer.

Configuration Management is also required at the project level. Some products will be shared across two or more projects. It is essential that each project's Configuration Management process meets the requirements of the programme, as well as its own internal needs.

9.2.3 Responsibilities for Configuration Management

The Programme Manager will be responsible for designing the baselines appropriate to the programme, and identifying the relevant CIs with input from the Business Change Manager(s) and others who have responsibilities for delivering services and maintaining business continuity.

The Programme Office will typically be responsible for administering the Configuration Management process, maintaining copies of relevant documentation concerning the CIs, and controlling the release of CIs following appropriate approvals.

Responsibilities for reviewing and approving the CIs need to be defined and allocated to individuals with appropriate skills and authority.

9.3 Assessing quality

Programmes are no different from other activities in that progress should be assessed at regular points and performance measured against required standards and preset criteria. The management processes used during a programme should be able to demonstrate that governance is effective and appropriate for the programme, that the particular needs of stakeholders are being – or are likely to be – met, and that the investment is delivering the required results. Reviews should be scheduled throughout the programme; as a minimum, at the end of each tranche.

Reviews can address a range of quality aspects, including:

- external scrutiny (audit, legal or regulatory)

- internal audit requirements

- peer review

- independent expert scrutiny (for example, Gateway Reviews)

- business assurance

- benefit realisation

- fitness for purpose assurance.

9.4 Audit reviews

Audit is a generic activity, not one confined solely to the audit of financial accounts, and is often used to assess the management and conduct of a programme. Audit involves examination of the activities of a programme with the aim of determining the extent to which they conform to accepted criteria. The criteria may be internal standards and procedures or external codes of practice, accounting standards, contract conditions or statutory requirements. Audit reviews may be carried out by internal audit staff or by external audit bodies.

Programme auditors should be able to provide the programme with particular information needs, and be able to assist the Programme Manager to build in any specific audit requirements to the governance procedures and plans for the programme.

Programme audits will consider any or all aspects of the programme, its management or delivery capability. In particular, audit reviews may focus on some specific areas such as:

- the embedding of risk management, including the active management of risks to delivery of benefits

- the interfaces with other programmes or initiatives within the organisation

- the exploitation and use of lessons learned from other programmes either within the organisation or elsewhere

- the consideration of realistic options in the delivery of the programme's objectives

- engagement with stakeholders, including pro-active consideration of their interests in the programme and the impact of the changes on them as individuals or groups, perhaps through piloting or trials

- contingency arrangements for dealing with the unexpected and ensuring continuity of business operations.

Some typical information management requirements that audit might need to be built into Programme Management are given below.

- What records and audit trails will be necessary to satisfy these requirements? The requirements may fall under categories of management decisions on policy, strategy and tactical approaches, transaction records, process control records or records of system use. The Programme Office will be responsible for administration of all information about the programme. It may be necessary to establish a specific role for the task of information management on large programmes.

- How long will it be necessary to retain such information? Contract documents, for example, may extend over a considerable period of time and may be required well after completion of the programme in the event of disputes.

- How are records to be recovered for audit scrutiny? Information management of programme documentation will require careful consideration about how to catalogue, file, store and retrieve information.

- Where programme records only exist in electronic form, how will their authenticity be demonstrated? It should not be assumed that electronic, as opposed to paper, records will form acceptable evidence to auditors.

- Are the Programme Management framework and processes adequately documented? Internal audit, in particular, will typically be concerned with providing senior management with assurance that the approach is functioning effectively. However, comprehensive and usable documentation about how the programme is being managed also provides a source of reference for all personnel involved in the programme.

9.5 Programme assurance

Assurance is a 'value-added' function for the programme, involving the assessment of specific aspects to generate confidence that the programme is being managed effectively and is on track to realise the expected benefits and achieve the desired outcomes. Assurance, like audit, should be carried out independently of the Programme Management Team. Assurance reviews may be focused on any number of aspects, for example:

- quality management assurance – assessing the implementation and performance of the programme according to the Quality Management Strategy

- business assurance – assessing the management of the Business Case and the continued viability of the programme against it

- stakeholder assurance – assessing the mechanisms and performance of the Stakeholder Management arrangements.

All Programme Management roles include a responsibility for assurance of that role's particular areas of interest, regardless of whether the programme will be subject to more formal audit scrutiny. For example, the Senior Responsible Owner will require assurance that the programme's Business Case is being managed appropriately and that it remains aligned with strategic objectives. The Programme Manager will need to be assured that the risk management activities are operating effectively, and the Business Change Manager that stakeholder issues are being managed effectively. The Programme Office may provide appropriately skilled resources for assurance reviews.

Part of developing the appropriate governance arrangements for the programme will involve considering what assurance functions should be applied:

- what is to be assured? (management processes, key programme documents, specific stakeholder requirements, for example)

- what skills and experience are required to be able to undertake the required assurance?

- how and when will assurance be undertaken for the programme as a whole and for the projects within it?

- what outputs will be required from the assurance function?

- how will the assurance function maintain an awareness of the changing environment in which the programme is operating?

Assurance reviews may be carried out by peer groups or other individuals from elsewhere in the organisation, or by specifically contracted personnel. There should be a clear brief for each assurance review. Assurance reviews may be carried out at any time during the programme, and should be repeated in areas where problems were identified and recommendations made for improvements.

9.6 Project assurance

Each of the projects are responsible for establishing appropriate mechanisms for assuring the quality of their progress and outputs. It may be useful for the programme to be involved in project-level reviews to provide assurance at the programme level that the projects remain aligned to their Business Cases, to the programme and its objectives. The Programme Office may be involved by providing the programme perspective during project level reviews. The Programme Manager and/or Business Change Manager(s) may also be involved in some of the more critical project-level reviews.

9.7 The Quality Management Strategy

The delivery of the programme's objectives and the ultimate achievement of the desired benefits and outcome(s) will involve a range of quality management activities. The Quality Management Strategy defines **what** criteria will be used to assess quality, **what** quality activities will be incorporated into the management and delivery of the programme, **who** will be responsible for carrying out these activities, and **how** the programme will meet required audit and organisational standards for quality assurance and quality control.

Programmes involving formal contracts with third parties for delivery of products or services to the programme will need to consider the relevant contractual requirements concerning quality management. Quality requirements specified in contracts should be consistent with the programme's overall Quality Management Strategy.

The Quality Management Strategy provides input to the planning of a programme to ensure the required resources and time commitments are built into the plans.

For further details about the Quality Management Strategy see Appendix B.

9.8 Responsibilities for quality management

The Senior Responsible Owner is ultimately accountable for all aspects of quality on the programme. This responsibility is discharged through the roles of Programme Manager, Business Change Manager(s), and the Programme Office as follows:

- the Programme Manager for the Quality Management Strategy, and the setting up, running and delivery of outputs from the Project Portfolio

- the Business Change Manager(s) for the implementation, transition, and realisation of benefits from the outputs

- the Programme Office for establishing and maintaining the programme's quality management activities. The Programme Office is also responsible for establishing the appropriate audit, assurance and review processes for the programme.

3 Programme Management lifecycle

This Part describes the activities, inputs, outputs, decisions and responsibilities throughout the lifecycle.

10 Overview of processes and products

Figure 10.1 shows the processes and key management products involved in Programme Management. Although shown in the figure as linear, each process may in reality require more than one iteration before the next one is begun. Having progressed to a later process, it is often necessary to return to the work of an earlier process for clarification or refinement of ideas and information.

The trigger for *Identifying a programme* is a Programme Mandate providing the high-level, strategic objectives of the programme. From the Programme Mandate, the objectives are developed into the Programme Brief. Formal approval of the Programme Brief is required from the Sponsoring Group and Senior Responsible Owner before the programme proceeds any further.

The Programme Brief (following approval) is the key input to *Defining a programme*. It provides the basis for development of the Programme Definition, the plans,

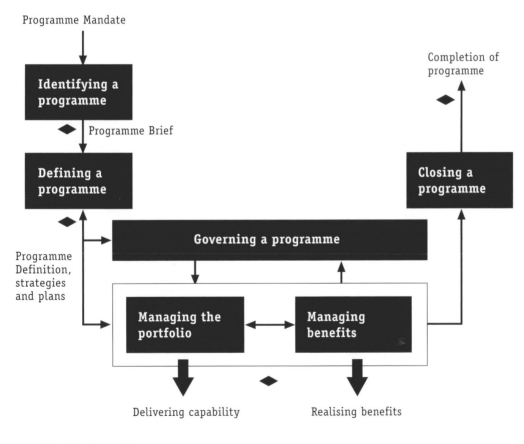

Figure 10.1 Programme Management processes and key products

and the strategies for programme governance. This information requires formal approval by the Senior Responsible Owner and Sponsoring Group before the programme is formally established.

The programme's governance arrangements are established and implemented in *Governing a programme*. The Programme Definition and plans are the basis for *Managing the portfolio* and *Managing benefits*.

The projects and activities are grouped into tranches. Each tranche delivers a step change in capability after which benefits realisation can be assessed. The activities of *Managing the portfolio* and *Managing benefits* are repeated for each tranche. The end of each tranche provides a major review point at which the programme can be formally assessed in terms of its progress towards achieving the desired outcomes and measurable realisation of benefits. Throughout the

programme, progress monitoring provides continual assessment of crucial questions such as, 'Are we still on track?', 'Is the Business Case still valid and relevant?', and 'Do we need to change anything to realign the programme?'

Closing a programme is done as the programme completes – when the Blueprint is delivered and the capabilities required to achieve the Vision Statement are implemented. Further reviews may be required following programme closure to assess and measure the continuing realisation of benefits.

10.1 Programme Management information

Information about the programme and how it is progressing is captured and maintained in a series of

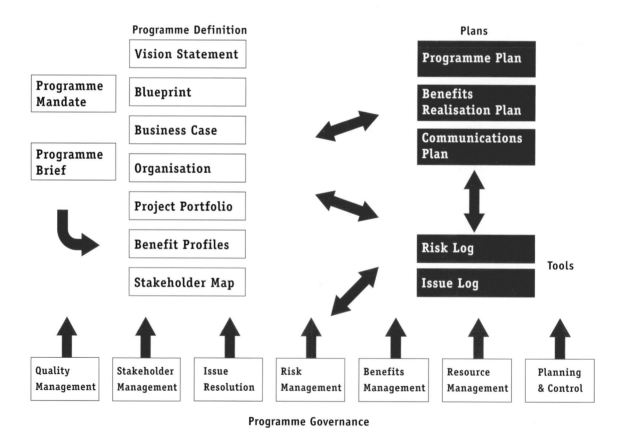

Figure 10.2 Inter-relating programme information

interrelated products. These products are essential for effective governance, monitoring progress, and satisfying audit requirements. The information created and used by the Programme Management Team will need to fit with organisational policies, standards and procedures (for example, SMART procurement). This guide refers to the information products shown in Figure 10.2, which shows how they link together.

The Programme Brief is the basis for developing the Programme Definition. The Programme Definition is the collection of information defining **what** the programme is going to deliver, **how** it will do it, **what** benefits to expect, **who** will be involved, and **how much** investment will be required.

The programme governance arrangements are defined as a series of strategies covering quality, stakeholders, issues, risks, benefits and resources. The planning and control aspects are included in the Programme Plan.

The Programme Definition provides the basis for developing the plans, namely the Programme Plan, the Benefits Realisation Plan and the Communications Plan. The Risk Register and Issue Log are used to support the ongoing management of the programme.

The information represented in Figure 10.2 is central to the effective management of the programme. The creation, subsequent updating and review of the information is summarised in Figure 10.3.

	Identifying a programme	Defining a programme	Governing a programme	Managing the portfolio	Managing Benefits	Closing a programme
Programme Mandate	CO					
Programme Brief	CR	RV				
Vision Statement	CR	RF			RV	RV
Blueprint		CR	RF	UP	UP	RV
Business Case		CR	RF	RV	RV	RV
Organisation		CR	IM			RV
Project Portfolio		CR	RF	RF	RF	RV
Benefit Profiles		CR	RF	RF	UP	RV
Stakeholder Map		CR	RF	RF	RF	RV
Planning and Control		CR	IM	RF	RF	RV
Resource Management		CR	IM	RF	RF	RV
Benefits Management		CR	IM	RF	RF	RV
Stakeholder Management		CR	IM	RF	RF	RV
Risk Management		CR	IM	RF	RF	RV
Issue Resolution		CR	IM	RF	RF	RV
Quality Management		CR	IM	RF	RF	RV
Programme Plan		CR	RF	UP	UP	RV
Benefits Realisation Plan		CR	RF	UP	UP	RV
Communications Plan		CR	RF	UP	UP	RV
Risk Log		CR	UP	UP	UP	RV
Issue Log		CR	UP	UP	UP	RV

CO	Confirmed	IM	Implemented
CR	Created	RV	Reviewed
RF	Refined	UP	Updated

Figure 10.3 Matrix of programme information and Programme Management processes

11 Identifying a programme

11.1 Summary and purpose

The strategy, initiative or policy that is driving the change process generates the Programme Mandate – the trigger for initiating the overall Programme Management process. The Programme Mandate acts as a point of reference for *Identifying a programme*, when the Programme Brief is developed. *Identifying a programme* is typically a short process, perhaps taking only a few weeks to complete. The Programme Brief begins to detail the benefits, costs, timescales and risks involved such that:

- the programme can be identified in terms of what it is being set up to achieve and what the desired benefits are for the organisation(s) and stakeholders involved

- a management decision can be made on whether the programme is desirable and appropriate, and whether to commit the investment and resources required to proceed to the next process of *Defining a programme*.

11.2 Activities

11.2.1 Sponsoring the programme

A programme requires top-level sponsorship in order to gain and maintain the necessary commitment to the investment, resources, timescales, delivery and impact of change that will be involved. Those senior executives who are responsible for delivering the strategic objectives or policy requirements of the organisation form the programme's Sponsoring Group. The Sponsoring Group provides the Programme Mandate.

The Sponsoring Group is made up of those senior exec-utives who have a strategic interest in the programme, typically including investment decision-making. Members of the Sponsoring Group are key stakeholders for the programme. Each member of the Sponsoring Group requires their particular interests and engage-ment with the programme to be defined. The members of the Sponsoring Group should then confirm their acceptance of, and commitment to, their roles.

11.2.2 Confirming the Programme Mandate

The Programme Mandate articulates the strategic objectives for the programme, optimum strategies for delivery, the improvements that are expected to result, and how the programme fits with other initiatives. This information sets the scene for a controlled startup for the programme and should be confirmed at its outset.

The Programme Mandate may be a documented output from the strategic planning or policy development process. However, it may not exist as a single, cohesive document. In this case, the concepts and objectives for the programme will need to be drawn together using facilitated workshops, interviews and discussions with the Sponsoring Group, key stakeholders, members of the organisation's executive and senior management teams.

The Programme Mandate defines the strategic require-ments of the programme and should clearly map back to the overall strategic plans of the organisation.

11.2.3 Appointing the Senior Responsible Owner

The Senior Responsible Owner will be the 'champion' for the programme and have ultimate accountability and personal responsibility for its successful outcome. Other titles are commonly used for this role – 'Programme Director', for example.

The Senior Responsible Owner should be the

appropriate senior level individual from the Sponsoring Group who has the required authority, credibility, experience and skills to lead and direct the programme.

The individual should be appointed as soon as possible during this process to provide leadership, direction and a focal point for the programme, particularly important during the initial identification and definition discussions.

11.2.4 Producing the Programme Brief

The Programme Brief provides the formal basis for assessing whether the proposed programme is viable and achievable. Using information from the Programme Mandate, the programme's specific objectives, required benefits, potential risks, outline costs and timescales are fleshed out. More detailed analysis of viable options for delivery can also be developed. The typical content of a Programme Brief is described in Appendix B.

The use of a Programme Brief (rather than a complete, highly detailed Business Case) at this early stage of a programme helps to avoid nugatory, and often time-consuming, work on detailed cost analysis, investment appraisals, expenditure profiles, and so on, when the overall concept of the proposed programme may not be viable for reasons other than financial justification. For example, if the initial expectations of benefit realisation are unlikely to be achieved within a sensible timeframe, is the proposed programme worth taking any further? Perhaps a different approach to achieving the desired outcomes would be worth exploring?

The more comprehensive the Programme Mandate, the less analysis and refinement work will be needed to develop the Programme Brief. However, programmes do tend to be major spenders. It is important to develop, at least in outline, the budget and funding requirements, as well as expenditure timescales, to provide sufficient information to support the management decision on whether to proceed to *Defining a programme*.

The Programme Brief (once approved) provides the basis for development of the programme's full Business Case and other Programme Management information.

11.2.5 Developing terms of reference for Programme Definition

Defining a programme involves the detailed planning and design of all aspects of the programme. Terms of reference for this work are produced, together with a plan for the amount of time and resources required.

It is essential to plan sufficient time and resources, and to identify individuals with the right skills and experience, for the development of a detailed Programme Definition. At this point in the life of a programme there will be much uncertainty and ambiguity over the detail of what the programme will involve. Planning sufficient time and resources for *Defining a programme* will help to clarify and reduce this uncertainty and ambiguity.

It may be helpful to identify and involve the likely Programme Manager during this process. Early involvement will help to build commitment from the individual who will be tasked with executing the programme.

11.2.6 Review

It is useful to conduct a formal review of the Programme Brief to assess the scope, rationale and objectives of the programme. The review should assess the extent to which the organisation(s) involved have the capacity and capability to deliver and realise the expected benefits. The risks identified and any critical assumptions that have been made should be challenged. The review may involve an internal peer group or external independent scrutiny (such as a Gateway Review).

11.2.7 Approval to proceed

The Programme Brief, the terms of reference and the plan for *Defining a programme* require the formal approval of the Senior Responsible Owner and Sponsoring Group. This approval is based on a confirmed understanding of, and commitment to, the proposed programme's vision, and the preliminary view of its expected benefits, risks, issues, timescales, resources and costs (all contained within the Programme Brief). There must be clear justification for the investment of resources in the programme, and the estimated benefits must outweigh the (managed) risks.

11.3 Inputs, outputs and decisions

Table 11.1 summarises the inputs, outputs and decisions associated with *Identifying a programme*.

11.4 Responsibilities

Table 11.2 summarises the responsibilities for the activities involved in *Identifying a programme*.

Table 11.1 Inputs, outputs and decisions for *Identifying a programme*

Item	Type	Notes
Programme Mandate	Input	The trigger for *Identifying a programme* that defines the overall objectives for the programme
Programme Brief	Output	Provides the basis for deciding whether the programme is justified
Terms of reference and plan for *Defining a programme*	Output	Description of the scope and resources required to deliver the detailed Programme Definition
Appointment of the Senior Responsible Owner	Output	Appointed from within the Sponsoring Group
Approval to proceed or reconsider	Decision	Approval, endorsement and commitment from the Senior Responsible Owner and the Sponsoring Group to proceed, or to consider another course of action

Table 11.2 Roles and responsibilities for *Identifying a programme*

Role	Responsibilities
Senior Responsible Owner	Directing the development of the Programme Brief, terms of reference and plan for Programme Definition (this work may require a small team). Close liaison with other members of the Sponsoring Group. Commissioning a review to provide assurance on the Programme Brief. Approval of the Programme Brief and commitment to proceed to *Defining a programme*
Sponsoring Group	Providing and approving the Programme Mandate and giving their commitment to the programme. Approval of the Programme Brief and commitment to proceed to *Defining a programme*

12 Defining a programme

12.1 Summary and purpose

Defining a programme is a crucial process for a programme. It is where the detailed definition and planning for the programme is done and it provides the basis for deciding whether to proceed with the programme or not.

The Programme Brief is used as the starting point for refining the programme's objectives and targets into the Programme Definition, which defines what the programme is going to do, how it is going to do it, who is involved, and the Business Case for the programme. The governance framework for the programme is developed, which defines the strategies for quality, stakeholders, issues, risks, benefits, resources and planning and control. The plans are developed providing information on the resources, dependencies and timescales for delivery and realisation of benefits.

The inevitable trade-off between resources, costs, quality, timings and benefits requires agreement between the Sponsoring Group and Senior Responsible Owner. Formal approval is required from the Sponsoring Group and Senior Responsible Owner to proceed with the programme. This approval will be conditional on whether the programme presents a sound basis for the investment.

12.2 Activities

12.2.1 Establishing the team to define the programme

The Senior Responsible Owner will typically require the support of a small team to help develop the Programme Definition, the governance strategies and plans for the programme. The terms of reference produced in *Identifying a programme* are used to select and appoint the team. The team will need appropriate background, skills, knowledge and experience in areas relevant to the programme and its management. Members of the team may subsequently fulfil formal roles within the programme organisation structure. It may be helpful to appoint the Programme Manager to assist the Senior Responsible Owner in these early stages of definition.

12.2.2 Developing the Vision Statement

The information contained in the Programme Brief is refined into the programme's Vision Statement. The Vision Statement describes what the desired outcome(s) are. It provides the basis for communicating and encouraging the buy-in and commitment from stakeholders.

The Vision Statement is also used to give the programme a clear statement of direction. The following examples illustrate the business-led emphasis that should be reflected in the Vision Statement:

This organisation will facilitate and promote the development of a greater range of relevant higher education courses that encourages an x% increase in the intake of HE students over the next three years.

This organisation will deliver HR services to departments in a way that reduces the departments' ongoing recruitment costs by x% per head year on year.

For further details on the Vision Statement see Appendix B.

12.2.3 Developing the Blueprint

The Blueprint is a model of the business or organisation, its working practices and processes, the information it requires and the technology that will be needed to deliver the capabilities described in the Vision Statement. The Blueprint is developed during this process; however, it may need further refinement as the level of understanding about the programme is increased. The Blueprint is used throughout the programme to maintain the focus on delivery of the new capability.

Developing the Blueprint involves many concepts of organisational design. It may encompass all dimensions of the organisation or business – its cultural aspects as well as its structure – and how they need to change. Business analysis and design techniques may also be required to explore fully the opportunities and options for achieving the capabilities described in the Vision Statement. There are typically many options for achieving the required changes, with associated variations in costs and impact. Exploring these options and assessing the implications on the investment required is an important aspect for designing the optimum Blueprint for the programme. This work may be carried out as a feasibility study or small project in its own right.

The key drivers behind the Blueprint are the benefits and outcomes required. The scope of change defined in the Blueprint should remain closely aligned to the required benefits and not start to 'creep' to embrace other (albeit beneficial) changes that could distract the programme from achieving its true objectives.

Designing the Blueprint to realise the required benefits needs to be balanced against the costs of realising those benefits. The programme's Business Case is developed in parallel with the Blueprint to ensure consistency between the proposed changes to the organisation, the costs of making the changes, and realistic realisation of the benefits required.

Involving the target business community, who will be part of the 'new' organisation, in the development of the Blueprint is a powerful method for improving the quality of the information and increasing the sense of ownership and buy-in to the change.

For further details on the Blueprint see Appendix B.

12.2.4 Developing the Benefit Profiles

The Vision Statement and Programme Brief identify the required benefits from the programme. Each benefit (and dis-benefit) requires a complete definition, known as a Benefit Profile. Each Benefit Profile should cover:

- a description of what the benefit is

- its relationship with other benefits

- when it will be realised

- what measures and performance indicators will be used to assess achievement levels and their costs

- what aspects of the Blueprint are required in order for this benefit to be realised

- which project(s) or activity is directly related to realisation of this benefit

- dependencies on other parts of the programme, or on risks

- who will be responsible for ensuring the successful realisation of this benefit.

The total set of Benefit Profiles provides a planning and control tool to track progress on the delivery and realisation of the benefits. The Benefit Profiles will be further refined as the detailed definition of the programme is developed. For further details on Benefit Profiles see Chapter 4.

12.2.5 Validating the benefits

A realistic assessment of the inevitable trade-off between the cost of realising and measuring the benefit against the value of having that benefit should be made, so that the problems associated with aiming to realise unrealistic benefits can be avoided.

Each benefit should represent some aspect of the programme's desired outcomes. Benefits that are not linked to strategic objectives may actually be unhelpful; furthermore, they may distract from achieving the real outcomes.

Benefit Profiles should be able to pass four critical tests:

- **description** – what precisely is this benefit?

- **observation** – what differences should be noticeable between pre- and post-programme implementation?

- **attribution** – where will this benefit arise?

- **measurement** – how will the achievement of the benefit be measured?

12.2.6 Identifying the stakeholders

All the programme's stakeholders should be identified, together with their particular interest in the programme (see Chapter 5). It is also important to identify any stakeholders who are likely to be worse off as a result of the programme, as their interests and influence may prevent the programme's successful outcome.

The analysis of stakeholders will identify the various information needs and communication flows that should be established as part of programme communications. A Stakeholder Map showing the various stakeholders and their particular interests in the programme is a useful way to capture and manage information about a large number of stakeholders. For further details on identifying and analysing stakeholders see Chapter 5.

12.2.7 Designing the Project Portfolio

The Blueprint and the Benefit Profiles provide the basis for identifying the projects and any other activities necessary to deliver the new capabilities expressed in the Vision Statement. These projects and activities form the programme's Project Portfolio. The Project Portfolio represents the programme's approach to delivery of the outcome(s) and realisation of the benefits. It is used as the basis for developing the Programme Plan. More detailed project delineation and planning may be required once the programme has been formally approved.

There may be different options for achieving target improvements or changes in business operations, in which case these should be explored in terms of timing, content, risks and benefits. Some projects and activities may be existing, ongoing work that will need to be adopted into the programme as part of the Project Portfolio; alternatively they may be new initiatives that will require commissioning by the programme at the appropriate point. Where the Portfolio consists of a large number of separate projects, there may be opportunities to bring some together where the nature of the work or potential synergies might prove beneficial.

The Project Portfolio should include the following information about each project:

- a description of the project, including its outputs and timescales

- its dependencies with other projects

- the contribution it will make to benefit realisation.

One of the objectives of designing the Project Portfolio is to place clear and direct accountability on the projects, while avoiding a spaghetti-like tangle of interdependencies. This can be achieved by ensuring that the delineation of project boundaries maximises the internal consistency of the projects (sometimes referred to as 'cohesion') and minimises the number of interfaces and dependencies between the projects (sometimes referred to as 'coupling'). This enables project interdependencies to be managed more effectively. It may also identify changes to existing projects such that they are better aligned to the programme's objectives.

The following may help delineation of the projects:

- delineating by **discipline** – programmes are typically multidisciplinary, whereas projects are often seen as single discipline. Projects can be defined and scoped such that each involves a single discipline

- delineating by **location** – multi-site projects are inherently difficult to manage, largely because of the communication overheads between members of the project teams. Projects may be scoped by grouping activities that can be achieved on a single site

- delineating by **outputs** – projects may be defined such that each is responsible for a single set of outputs, or outputs that are closely related.

Delineating projects requires pragmatism. Reducing dependencies is just as important as defining clearly manageable projects.

There may be project activity outside the scope of the programme that could conflict with the programme's objectives. These should be identified and any possible conflicts defined so that appropriate action can be taken if required.

12.2.8 Identifying tranches

The outcome(s) described in the Vision Statement can rarely be delivered in a single pass; it will typically be reached through progressive refinements or step changes in the capabilities of the organisation. These step changes can be used to define the end of successive tranches where formal reviews can be carried out.

The projects and activities in the Project Portfolio are scheduled together showing their relative timescales and dependencies. The schedule is grouped into tranches reflecting the step changes in capability. It may not be possible to define all of the required projects fully at this point. Further analysis may be required to complete the scoping of later projects after the results of a first set of enabling projects (such as

improving communications or improving competencies) have been assessed. For further details on scheduling and tranches see Chapter 7.

12.2.9 Designing the programme's organisation structure

The organisation structure for directing, managing, controlling and supporting the programme is designed. Successful programme delivery requires sufficient resourcing of the Programme Management activities. The structure must allow effective decision-making and efficient communication flows around the various members of the programme team. The nature and size of the programme will influence the design of an appropriate organisation structure. The structure will need to integrate with, and operate alongside, the existing management structures of the organisation(s). The organisation structure should reflect the management levels appropriate to the visibility and significance of the programme.

Each role within the organisation structure should be defined with its specific accountabilities, responsibilities, and tasks, together with the relevant skills and competencies required. Individuals with the appropriate skills and experience who can take on these roles should be identified.

Many individuals assigned to programme roles will also be doing 'business as usual'. Prioritisation of workloads is an important management consideration. The amount of work required for each role needs to be balanced against the amount of time the individual is realistically able to provide. It may be necessary to procure external resources for the programme organisation, thus providing more experienced and specialist skills to fulfil some of the roles. It is important to remember that procurement is typically a lengthy and specification-driven process; sufficient time and resources should be planned for procurement and contract management activities.

For further details on programme organisation see Chapter 3.

12.2.10 Developing the programme's Business Case

The Business Case brings together information about the programme covering the costs, benefits, timings and risks, so that the overall value for money and achievability of the programme can be assessed and appropriate management decisions made about the viability of the programme.

The level of detail required in the Business Case will depend on the particular programme and its business environment. It is useful to keep the level of detail on benefits the same as the level of detail on costs to prevent any bias arising simply because more (or less) is known about particular benefits. The level of detail will also reflect the amount of uncertainty there is surrounding the programme. The Business Case should be developed with as much information as is known or available at this point, and should make clear the level of confidence in the estimates to enable a balanced decision on benefits versus costs versus risks to be made.

For further details on the Business Case see Chapter 8.

12.2.11 Developing the programme's governance arrangements

The programme's governance arrangements should cover how the programme is going to handle the inevitable interdependencies and bring all the different aspects together. The various strategies required are described below.

12.2.11.1 Benefits management

Benefits management activities and responsibilities define what needs to be done and who is involved in order to ensure the identified benefits will actually be realised. A Benefits Management Strategy is produced describing the functions, roles and responsibilities for benefit planning and realisation. It also describes the measurement, assessment and review processes for monitoring benefit realisation. The development of the Benefits Management Strategy needs to be carried out in close alignment with the Vision Statement, Blueprint and the Business Case to ensure the structure and objectives of the programme and its activities are going to realise the benefits expected and to achieve the outcomes desired. For further details on benefits management see Chapter 4.

12.2.11.2 Stakeholder Management

A Stakeholder Management Strategy is developed to define how the programme will engage with all stakeholder groups and what information flows will be established and maintained during the programme. For further details on Stakeholder Management see Chapter 5.

12.2.11.3 Risk management and issue resolution

Risks are things that may happen at some point in the future and require positive management to reduce their likelihood of happening or their impact on the programme, or both. Issues are things happening now that are affecting the programme in some way and need to be actively dealt with and resolved. Risks, should they occur, turn into issues. Strategies for handling both risks and issues are developed.

The Risk Management Strategy defines how risks to the programme will be identified, analysed, monitored, and controlled. It should also encompass the processes required for the management of risks on projects within the Project Portfolio and should define how any project risks that affect other parts of the programme will be escalated, managed and controlled.

The Issue Resolution Strategy defines how issues will be captured, assessed, resolved and communicated. As with risk management, procedures for issue management at the project level need to be integrated at the programme level. Resolving issues on programmes often involves handling complex problems that impact across the entire programme. Escalation routes to senior levels must be efficient and effective.

It is essential to have the Risk Register and Issue Log held centrally to support the necessary proactive management processes across the programme. Both logs should be created as early as possible, since risks and issues will already be emerging.

For further details on risk management and issue resolution see Chapter 6.

12.2.11 4 Quality management

A Quality Management Strategy is developed to define the approach the programme will take to ensure that quality is built into all aspects of the programme from the outset. It should also cover how quality will be assured in the programme's deliverables, and by whom. The Programme Plan should include details of when activities relating to managing quality will be undertaken. For further details on managing quality see Chapter 9.

12.2.11.5 Planning and control

The planning and control information and the arrangements for monitoring progress of the programme are developed and included in the Programme Plan. For further details see Chapters 7 and 8.

12.2.11.6 Resource management

A Resource Management Strategy is developed to identify the resources required for the programme and defining how they will be acquired and managed. Resources will include finances, people, assets and technology. For further details on managing resources see Chapter 7.

12.2.12 Developing the Communications Plan

The Communications Plan for the programme should cover information flows outward (from the programme) and inward (into the programme). The programme will need input from stakeholders to inform and influence the programme during its design and implementation. The Communications Plan indicates when, what, how, and with whom, information flows between the programme and its stakeholders will be established and maintained.

In addition to information about change and the implications for the programme, there is a wide range of subject material to be communicated in any programme, for example:

- Programme Management organisation and arrangements

- people; their in-programme and outside-programme activities

- goals and objectives

- policies, strategies, plans

- process and transitional issues impacting stakeholders

- promotion, training and expectation management

- achievements, challenges, successes and failures.

For further details on the Communications Plan see Chapter 5.

12.2.13 Developing the Benefits Realisation Plan

The Benefit Profiles are used to develop an overall Benefits Realisation Plan showing how the total set of benefits will be realised. The Benefits Realisation Plan should show the benefits will be achievable following the delivery of new capability from the projects within the Project Portfolio. The tranches identified where step changes in capability will be delivered also signal potential 'early wins' from realising benefits. Priorities for benefit delivery should be considered to maximise opportunities for these early benefits.

The realisation of benefits must be allocated appropriate 'ownership' to ensure there is visible and demonstrable commitment from senior management. The 'owners' of the benefits will need to contribute to and endorse the Benefits Realisation Plan. The Benefits Realisation Plan and the Programme Plan are closely linked plans and may be combined into one plan showing projects' and transition plans together with benefit realisation activities (see Chapter 4).

12.2.14 Developing the Programme Plan

The Programme Plan is developed by bringing together the information on projects, resources, timescales, monitoring and control. The amount of information available and the level of detail required will develop as the programme progresses. An outline programme schedule showing the estimated relative timescales for the projects should be developed at this stage. It should identify the tranches where formal reviews of progress and benefits realisation can be carried out. For further details on developing the Programme Plan see Chapter 7.

12.2.15 Approval to proceed

The complete set of documentation describing the programme, its governance arrangements, plans, and Business Case should be approved by the Senior Responsible Owner before a formal endorsement from the programme's Sponsoring Group to confirm that the programme is designed to meet their expectations and requirements. The Sponsoring Group must give their approval to proceed, including their commitment to the investment required for the programme. This approval

should be based on the successful outcome of a formal review. Reviews may involve external independent scrutiny, such as a Gateway Review (see Chapter 9).

On many programmes, it may not be possible to clarify the total investment at this point. In this situation, the approval could be to proceed only to the end of the first tranche, at which point further formal approvals would be required and more detailed information would be available.

12.3 Inputs, outputs and decisions

Table 12.1 summarises the inputs, outputs and decisions associated with *Defining a programme*.

12.4 Responsibilities

Table 12.2 summarises the responsibilities for the activities involved in *Defining a programme*.

Table 12.1 Inputs, outputs and decisions for *Defining a programme*

Item	Type	Notes
Programme Brief	Input	Approved by the Sponsoring Group at the end of *Identifying a programme*
Risk Register and Issue Log	Output	Created to capture currently known issues and risks and set in place appropriate management actions
The Programme Definition containing:	Output	
Vision Statement		Describing the 'end goal' of the programme
Blueprint		Describing the capabilities of the transformed organisation in its future 'state'
Business Case		A key programme document balancing the programme's benefits against costs and risks
Organisation structure		Tailored organisation structure, with roles and responsibilities for directing, managing, and delivering the programme
Project Portfolio		The list of projects and related activities involved in the programme
Benefit Profiles		Control tools for tracking the progress of each benefit (and dis-benefit) identified
Stakeholder Map		Showing all stakeholder groups and their specific interests in the work and outcomes from the programme
The governance arrangements defined in:	Output	
Benefits Management Strategy		Defining how the benefits will be managed, from identification to realisation
Stakeholder Management Strategy		Defining how stakeholders will be engaged throughout the programme
Issue Resolution Strategy		Defining the programme's governance arrangements for handling issues and changes
Risk Management Strategy		Defining the programme's governance arrangements for managing risks
Quality Management Strategy		Defining the programme's governance arrangements for managing quality
Resource Management Strategy		Defining the programme's resource requirements and how they will be acquired and managed

Table 12.1 Inputs, outputs and decisions for *Defining a programme* (continued)

Item	Type	Notes
Plans consisting of:	Output	
Benefits Realisation Plan		Showing the schedule of benefits realisation throughout the programme
Communications Plan		Showing the schedule of communications activities with stakeholders throughout the programme
Programme Plan		The major planning and control information about the programme. Includes governance arrangements for monitoring and control
Approval to proceed or stop	Decision	Formal commitment from the Sponsoring Group to proceed, stop or realign the programme

Table 12.2 Roles and responsibilities for *Defining a programme*

Role	Responsibilities
Senior Responsible Owner	Overall responsibility for directing the work of developing the Programme Definition, the governance arrangements and plans, and for providing the interface with the Sponsoring Group and other key stakeholders. The Senior Responsible Owner is also responsible for managing and monitoring any strategic risks facing the programme
Team appointed to develop the Programme Definition	Assisting the Senior Responsible Owner to define and capture all the information about the programme
Sponsoring Group	Endorsement of, and commitment to, the programme

13 Governing a programme

13.1 Summary and purpose

The purpose of *Governing a programme* is to establish and implement the governance arrangements for the programme. 'Governance' (as used in this guide) means the functions, processes and procedures that define how the programme is set up, managed and controlled.

Programmes involve a substantial amount of change for individuals, staff, operations, support services and the business environment in which the organisation(s) is operating. Governance arrangements need to be established to provide a framework for this upheaval and transformation. Programme governance provides the 'backdrop' for all activities of managing the programme and achieving the programme's outcomes.

13.2 Activities

13.2.1 Setting up the programme organisation

The organisation structure for the programme is implemented together with the formal appointment of the Programme Manager (if not appointed already). The other individuals identified as part of the organisation structure for the programme should also be appointed; in particular, the staff for the Programme Office. Each role should have a clearly defined set of responsibilities that the appointed individual accepts.

The selection and appointment procedures should include defining the skills and competencies required for each of the roles and carrying out a skills assessment for individuals nominated for the roles. Training and mentoring services from expert resources, either internal or external to the programme, should address any gaps in experience.

13.2.2 Setting up the Programme Office

The Programme Office should provide an 'information hub' for the programme and may also have skilled resources able to provide consultancy-style assistance to the Programme Management Team and the projects, as required. The Programme Office functions and procedures are established and operated throughout the programme.

13.2.3 Supporting governance requirements

The Programme Office provides support for the governance requirements of the programme; for example, collecting performance information to support progress monitoring. The various governance strategies define the required arrangements, information and procedures that need to be put in place. In particular, the funding arrangements need to be established and the accounting procedures implemented.

The standards for managing risks and issues, and for reporting progress, should be defined and implemented across the programme. The integration of project-level information, including risks and issues, needs to be established to enable reporting to be standardised across the programme. The quality systems defined in the Quality Management Strategy should be implemented.

13.2.4 Setting up the physical programme environment

The physical programme environment, including buildings, office space, office facilities and services, should be established. This may involve procuring or leasing appropriate facilities, or redeploying facilities from other areas within the organisation as defined in the Resource Management Strategy.

The technology and tools required to support the programme also need to be acquired and implemented, and staff trained in their use.

Typical tools used to support the programme include:

- Intranet and/or Internet websites

- planning, estimating and scheduling tools

- tools to support risk management, quality management, financial management, and change control

- document management and record management tools.

13.2.5 Risk management and issue resolution

The programme's overall risk profile needs to be continually monitored for changes affecting the impact or probability of identified risks. The Risk Register and Issue Log are reviewed and updated throughout the programme. Resolving issues and implementing the appropriate risk management activities are continued throughout the programme.

13.2.6 HR management

The Resource Management Strategy identifies the Human Resources (HR) requirements that need to be established. Programmes involving substantial changes affecting the working environment for staff will inevitably require extensive input from HR to assist with the redeployment and retraining of staff. There may be requirements for negotiations with trade unions representing the interests of employees' pay and conditions of working. For further details on the HR aspects see Chapter 3.

13.2.7 Procurement and contract management

The Resource Management Strategy identifies the requirements for procurement and contract management procedures for any procuring activities within the programme. These are set up. The programme may require the involvement of dedicated teams with appropriate skills and competencies to run procurements and contract and supplier management activities. Managing suppliers and maintaining alignment of their activities with the overall direction of the programme requires specific management attention and intervention if things go off track. Procurement and contract management activities must be defined within corporate policies and standards that may require tailoring to suit the particular needs of the programme.

13.2.8 Programme communications

The Communications Plan defines the channels the programme will use to inform the stakeholders about the programme and to encourage feedback into the programme. The required mechanisms are set up for communicating to all the identified stakeholders in the programme. It is useful to begin using the programme's communication channels as early as possible by providing details to the stakeholders of all the individuals appointed to specific roles on the programme. Thereafter, the communication activities should ensure the stakeholders are kept informed and engaged in the work of the programme. It is vital to maintain communications across the programme and with stakeholders about project progress, the benefits expected from the programme and their subsequent realisation.

13.2.9 Reporting, monitoring and control

Procedures and responsibilities for reporting, monitoring and control defined in the Programme Plan are implemented. Regular progress reporting from the project level informs the formal progress monitoring which keeps the programme on track. Monitoring progress may identify problem areas requiring management intervention. These issues should be escalated and actioned as soon as possible to prevent the programme losing momentum and moving off track.

A key aspect of control is ensuring the Blueprint and the delivery of new capabilities defined within it remain internally consistent and coherent. Programmes involving major technical infrastructures may require a dedicated design authority function.

Reporting arrangements, information content and frequencies will differ from one programme to another. The Programme Manager and Senior Responsible Owner should agree the reporting arrangements that keep both fully informed without over-burdening them with too much information.

13.2.10 Information management

The programme information is updated, refined and maintained as the programme progresses. At a minimum, this should be done at the end of each tranche. Successive refinements to the Blueprint will highlight any adjustments that may need to be made to the Project Portfolio to keep the programme on track. The Programme Plan and Benefits Realisation Plan should be refined as actual completion and delivery dates from the projects are known.

13.2.11 End-of-tranche reviews

As a minimum, the programme's Business Case, benefits and the benefits management process should be reviewed at the end of each tranche. At least one review should also be planned for after the programme has closed, to assess the realisation of benefits 'post-programme'. The end-of-tranche reviews may also include a formal assessment of the effectiveness of the Programme Management activities.

It may be useful to consider the assessment of benefits from both an 'internal' and 'external' perspective. The internal perspective will involve measuring reduction in costs, for example. The external perspective, for example, via a programme audit function, will involve assessing whether the potential for realisation of benefits remains on track and ensuring all the possible benefit dependencies are considered.

The following questions may help structure a benefit review:

- which planned benefits have been realised? If they have been realised, were the targets correct or should they have been increased?

- which planned benefits have not been realised? Why were they not realised? Can remedial action be taken to realise them or has the opportunity been lost?

- is there a pattern to the success/failure that can be used to inform other realisation plans?

- were the assumptions on which the realisation of the benefits was based correct? If not, what effect did this have on the realisation process?

- were there any unexpected benefits that have resulted? If so, can they now be planned and maximised further?

- have the dis-benefits been managed and minimised?

- were there any unexpected dis-benefits? If so, how can these be managed and minimised?

- are there any further potential benefits?

- do the measures applied appear to be the correct ones? Do they need changing or refining? Was the process of data collection to establish the measures effective?

The findings of each of the reviews should be disseminated to the rest of the programme.

13.2.12 Maintaining 'business as usual'

Whilst the programme is ongoing, the existing business operations need to be sustained. The technical integrity of systems and services needs to be maintained throughout the programme. As the projects are completed and transition activities get underway, the existing operations need either to be transferred to a new way of working, or be replaced with a new operation. Maintaining continuous services during the upheaval associated with change requires careful consideration and planning.

13.3 Inputs, outputs and decisions

Table 13.1 summarises the inputs, outputs and decisions associated with *Governing a programme*.

13.4 Responsibilities

Table 13.2 summarises the responsibilities for the activities involved in *Governing a programme*.

Table 13.1 Inputs, outputs and decisions for *Governing a programme*

Item	Type	Notes
Programme Definition	Input	Used to implement the programme organisation, roles and responsibilities, the Programme Office function, progress reporting and Business Case management arrangements
Programme Plan and Benefits Realisation Plan	Input	Used to monitor progress and measure performance
Governance strategies	Input	Used to implement the appropriate level of governance for the programme
Communications Plan	Input	Used to implement the communications with stakeholders throughout the programme
Risk Register	Output	Used to capture, monitor and track risks
Issue Log	Output	Used to capture, assess and resolve issues
HR and procurement standards	Output	Adhering to corporate standards
IT and support tools	Output	The technology infrastructure to support the programme
Progress reporting	Output	Reporting progress across the programme against plans
End-of-tranche reviews	Decision	Formal review and assessment of programme against its strategic objectives. Management decision to proceed, realign or potentially abandon the programme

Table 13.2 Roles and responsibilities for *Governing a programme*

Role	Responsibilities
Senior Responsible Owner	Appointment of Programme Manager and Business Change Manager(s) and ensuring the other roles defined in the programme organisation are appointed. Leading the ongoing monitoring and review activities of the programme, including commissioning formal reviews such as Gateways if required. Communicating with key stakeholders. Managing key strategic risks facing the programme. Providing direction to the Programme Manager and Business Change Manager(s) as required
Programme Manager	Responsible for establishing and managing the appropriate governance arrangements for the programme. Monitoring and managing progress against the Blueprint, Programme Plan and the Business Case. Updating the key programme documentation such as the Business Case. Ensuring the overall integrity of the programme is maintained. Managing the programme's risk management and issue resolution activities
Business Change Manager(s)	Maintaining 'business as usual' during the change process until transition and handover is complete. Also providing input to the reviews
Programme Office	Establishing and operating the programme's information management systems, reporting procedures, updating documentation, infrastructure, support tools, Configuration Management, change control and other procedures for the programme

14 Managing the portfolio

14.1 Summary and purpose

Managing the portfolio covers the activities for co-ordinating and managing project delivery according to the Programme Plan. Delivery from the Project Portfolio provides the new capabilities described in the Blueprint. The activities of *Managing the portfolio* are repeated for each tranche of the programme.

Managing the portfolio and *Managing benefits* are distinct processes, but they need to work closely together to harmonise the programme objectives with project delivery and benefit realisation.

14.2 Activities

14.2.1 Project startup

The Programme Manager is responsible for commissioning projects within the Project Portfolio and should ensure that appropriate individuals are appointed to the key project roles, such as Project Senior Responsible Owner (or 'Executive') and Project Manager. The project is accountable to the programme for its successful completion within specified time, cost and quality parameters. Tolerance levels may be set to enable the project delivery teams to manage minor deviations independently from the programme.

As each project is about to begin, the Programme Manager should ensure each project management team fully understands the project brief and has the appropriate project management standards in place. The project brief should provide a clear scope and a measurable definition of its required outputs.

The project brief should include:

- Project Definition, covering objectives, scope, outputs, constraints and interfaces

- Business Case covering cost and resource profiles, and Benefit Profile(s) detailing the benefits relevant to the project

- target delivery date

- quality expectations and acceptance criteria

- any risks identified at programme level relevant to the project.

In addition, the dependencies on other projects within the Project Portfolio should be defined so that the project is clearly positioned within the context of the programme.

14.2.2 Aligning projects with benefits realisation

The Business Change Manager is responsible for ensuring the particular benefits relevant to each project can be realised from implementation of the outputs from those projects. The particular project brief, the relevant Benefit Profile(s) and the Benefits Realisation Plan should be refined as part of project startup activities.

14.2.3 Aligning projects with programme objectives

For projects that are already underway, their progress and project information (such as the Project Initiation Document) is reviewed with the project teams. Any required amendments, rescoping or replanning, in order to align with the programme's Blueprint,

Programme Plan and Benefits Realisation Plan should be agreed and actioned.

14.2.4 Monitoring progress

The Programme Office should provide assistance to the projects in the development of their plans and progress reporting to the programme. Project reports should contain relevant highlight information in a standardised format to help aggregate the information at the programme level.

Progress against the Programme Plan is monitored and tracked, using information provided by the projects. Any departures from previously published project plans are assessed for impact on the rest of the programme. The impact of any change within a project or on other parties within the programme needs to be recognised as early as possible in order to manage the change carefully.

The 'live' projects are monitored by focusing on the areas that are key to the programme, such as:

* **outputs** – it is vital that the project outputs meet the requirements of their 'customers', which in some cases will be the programme itself. This may be handled through quality or assurance reviews

* **timely completion** – each project must take responsibility for adhering to timely forecasts of delivery and working within the tolerances set. This is required especially for outputs supplied to other projects, which will be affected by any slippages against plans. Any likely exceeding of tolerances should be reported as early as possible to the programme level, typically via exception reports

* **risks, issues and assumptions** – projects within a programme comprise a mutually dependent network. It is important for the integrity of this network that project teams are open and honest about risks and issues. Assumptions made at the project level can turn into risks at the programme level. A failure to recognise and track these could

jeopardise both other projects and the benefits expected from the programme

* **estimates** – the accuracy with which resource and cost estimating is carried out may be an important influence on the programme's Business Case. It may also affect other projects, for example, by reducing the level of shared resources unexpectedly

* **costs and benefits** – tolerance tracking of project costs and contribution towards benefit realisation is required

* **resources** – for example, checking for sufficient levels of funding, availability, staff numbers, skills, training, etc.

* **scope** – changes will inevitably occur, but they need to be formally managed under change control to avoid insidious scope creep.

14.2.5 Managing risks and resolving issues

The risks identified need to be regularly reviewed and challenged. New risks may be identified and activities to minimise probability or impact need to be actioned.

As the programme progresses there will be inevitable delays, unforeseen situations, and other issues which threaten the programme. The Programme Manager is responsible for recognising and dealing with anything that could affect the successful delivery of the programme. This may involve escalating problems to the Senior Responsible Owner, liaising with the Business Change Manager(s), or working with the projects to resolve problems that could affect project or benefit realisation.

14.2.6 Project closure

As each project prepares for closure, there should be a formal handover of the outputs to the programme. This signals the start of transition and integration of the outputs into business operations. Part of project closure involves the planning of a post-project review to assess the realisation of benefits from the project's outputs. These reviews should be scheduled to fit into the programme's review schedule and may require external independent scrutiny.

The process of project closure should include the dissemination of lessons learned across the programme to share knowledge and experiences with the other projects. It is often useful for members of the programme team to contribute to project evaluation review and 'lessons learned' reports where successes and problem areas associated with the project and its project management process are captured. Throughout the programme, the projects need to be advised of any issues arising that may impact on benefit responsibilities. The lessons learned reports may be useful to inform this activity.

14.2.7 Managing stakeholders

Maintaining the engagement of stakeholders and keeping them informed of progress and issues is an important part of successful Programme Management. The Communications Plan identifies the specific communication activities to be carried out. There will inevitably be trade-offs between one set of stakeholder interests and another. Co-operation and support will only be forthcoming if stakeholders have (and maintain) a good understanding about the programme and its progress, and feel that their individual perspectives are respected and considered.

Programme communications should be directed both outward, to gain support from the community whose

Table 14.1 Inputs, outputs and decisions for *Managing the portfolio*

Item	Type	Notes
Benefit Profiles and Benefits Realisation Plan	Input	Refined as projects are scoped and defined or redefined
Blueprint	Input	Updated and refined as projects deliver
Communications Plan	Input	Used to implement the communications activities and support the management of stakeholders and their expectations
Issue Log	Input	Used to capture and action issues affecting the programme
Programme Plan	Input	Updated and refined as projects deliver. The transition plan is also refined
Project progress reports	Input	For example, highlight reports, end stage reports. Used to monitor project progress and update Blueprint, Programme Plan and Benefits Realisation Plan
Risk Register	Input	Used to monitor risks associated with project delivery. Actively reviewed and updated as necessary
Project briefs	Output	For commissioning new projects
Project outputs	Output	The delivery from projects
Project lessons learned reports and project evaluation reviews	Output	Distributed across the programme for informing and improving management practices

operations will be affected by the changes the programme will bring about, and inward, to those establishing and implementing the programme. Open and informal internal communications help to build the identity and commitment of the personnel involved with managing the programme and its projects. Effective dialogue between all members of the Programme Management Team also assists the decision-making processes. Reliable, accurate and up-to-date information is essential to help balance the issues and priorities for the programme from a top-down perspective.

14.3 Inputs, outputs and decisions

Table 14.1 summarises the inputs, outputs and decisions associated with *Managing the portfolio*.

14.4 Responsibilities

Table 14.2 summarises the responsibilities for the activities involved in *Managing the portfolio*.

Table 14.2 Roles and responsibilities for *Managing the portfolio*

Role	Responsibilities
Programme Manager	Co-ordinating and integrating the work of the projects and managing the interdependencies. Progress monitoring against the Business Case, Programme Plan and Blueprint. Adjusting the Project Portfolio, Blueprint and plans to optimise benefit realisation. Managing stakeholder expectations and participating in communications activities to inform stakeholders of progress and issues
Business Change Manager	Ensuring the projects' outputs can be readily integrated into operational areas. Planning the transition within operational areas, accommodating requirements to maintain 'business as usual'
Project teams	Delivery of the projects to the programme; liaising with the Programme Office
Programme Office	Operating the programme information management system and providing support and guidance to the programme team and projects. Updating and maintaining programme information, providing advice as required. Progress reporting
Senior Responsible Owner	Monitoring progress across the programme at a strategic level and actioning management interventions where necessary. Ongoing advice and direction, resolving problems escalated by the Programme Manager. Resolution of issues escalated by the Programme Manager, approval of changes affecting the course of the programme. Maintaining the buy-in of the Sponsoring Group and other key stakeholders

15 Managing benefits

15.1 Summary and purpose

The purpose of *Managing benefits* is to track the benefits from their initial identification to their successful realisation. The activities cover monitoring the progress of the projects to ensure the outputs are fit for purpose and can be integrated into business operations such that the benefits can be realised.

Managing benefits also involves the planning and management of the transition from old to new ways of working while ensuring that 'business as usual' is maintained. The activities of this process are repeated as necessary for each tranche of the programme.

15.2 Activities

15.2.1 Establishing benefits measurements

In order to measure the improvements resulting from benefits realisation, the 'before' state needs to be measured. Without this there will be no way of assessing whether the 'after' measurements indicate an improvement or not.

Developing mechanisms for providing realistic and usable measures of benefit realisation is not straightforward. For some benefits, a simple financial measure such as increased revenue can be identified. For other benefits there may need to be a more complex form of measurement in order to demonstrate realisation of benefits. For example, using measurements of economy, efficiency and effectiveness (the 'three Es') can provide a set of assessments, which together form a view of benefit realisation.

For intangible benefits, where identifying a hard numerical measure is difficult, the measurement of realisation may involve developing a series of 'indicators' which together provide an assessment of improvement. These benefits may be assessed using customer satisfaction or perception surveys although care should be taken when relying on survey results as the data is dependent on the nature of the questions asked and the size of the group participating in the survey.

Measuring benefits obviously happens towards the end of the benefits management process. However, benefits realisation is what the programme is all about. It is important to ensure that benefits realisation is reinforced by the implementation of relevant measurement processes.

For further details on benefits management see Chapter 4.

15.2.2 Refining Benefit Profiles

The Benefit Profiles are managed and controlled throughout the programme with the same degree of rigour as costs. Both benefits and costs are of primary importance to the success of the programme. During the programme, there may be opportunities for improving the benefits so the Benefit Profiles will need to be reassessed and adjusted as necessary.

15.2.3 Benefits monitoring

Benefits may be realised from the changes made by individual projects or by a group of projects. Some projects may not realise benefits in their own right, but they will still require the same monitoring and tracking, as they may be providing prerequisites for other projects that will contribute to realisation of benefits.

Throughout the programme, progress is monitored against the Business Case, Programme Plan, Benefits Realisation Plan and the Blueprint, in particular to identify potential improvements to benefit achievement. Adjustments may be identified from a range of events or circumstances, including:

- business operations that will use the project outputs are unstable

- forward plans are no longer realistic based on experience to date

- external circumstances have changed affecting the future course of the programme

- the programme's objectives have changed or been refocused.

15.2.4 Transition management

As the projects approach completion, the relevant business operations need to be prepared for implementation of the outputs from the projects. The transition plan (part of the Programme Plan) is reviewed and updated to reflect the activities of transition. These activities need to be implemented and managed to ensure the business environment is ready to take on the new capability and also that appropriate levels of 'business as usual' are maintained.

The transition may be achieved in a single change to the operations, or may be achieved through a series of incremental or modular changes. The transition plan should provide the route map for implementation.

15.2.5 Supporting changes to culture and personnel

Managing the transition will often require careful consideration of individuals' personal concerns about their working environment and what the changes will mean to them. The transition to achieve the programme's outcome may affect individuals and organisations external to the organisation delivering the programme. HR support may be required to assist in the implementation of change.

15.2.6 Supporting benefit realisation

The embedding of new capability into the business such that it becomes 'business as usual' is where benefits realisation occurs. New ways of working will inevitably require a settling-down period. The Business Change Manager(s) should ensure the programme provides sufficient support during this period.

15.2.7 Measuring benefits

The Benefit Profiles define how each benefit will be measured and what the 'starting point' for this measurement activity was. Measuring benefit realisation

Table 15.1 Inputs, outputs and decisions for *Managing benefits*

Item	Type	Notes
Benefit Profiles and Benefits Realisation Plan	Input	Used to set up the measurement processes and capture the 'before' measurements as far as possible. Updated as programme progresses and used to measure realisation of benefits
Benefits Management Strategy	Input	Defines the overall measurement and management process
Business Case, Programme Plan and Blueprint, project progress reports	Input	Used to align projects, manage the transition and monitor the benefits
Improvements in operations and achievement of outcomes	Output	Measured improvements as a result of change

should be part of the end-of-tranche reviews. For further details on measuring benefits see Chapter 4.

15.3 Inputs, outputs and decisions

Table 15.1 summarises the inputs, outputs and decisions associated with *Managing benefits*.

15.4 Responsibilities

Table 15.2 summarises the responsibilities for the activities involved in *Managing benefits*.

Table 15.2 Roles and responsibilities for *Managing benefits*	
Role	**Responsibilities**
Business Change Manager	Responsible for benefits management. Managing the transition and implementation of project outputs, and realising the benefits through business change. Also responsible for refining and updating Benefit Profiles
Programme Manager	Maintaining risk management and issue resolution activities to ensure barriers to successful benefit realisation are removed/avoided
Programme Office	Collecting measurement data and reporting against Benefits Realisation Plan and Benefit Profiles
Senior Responsible Owner	Overall accountability for the realisation of benefits. Ongoing advice and direction, maintaining the buy-in of the Sponsoring Group and other key stakeholders

16 Closing a programme

16.1 Summary and purpose

Programmes tend to last for many months – typically, a few years. There is often a danger of allowing the programme to drift on, as if it is part of normal business. The purpose of *Closing a programme* is to ensure the focus is on achieving the end goal of the programme, formally recognising when the programme is completed and has delivered the required new capabilities described in the Blueprint. Benefits will have been realised during the running of the programme; however, some benefits, and possibly the majority of them, may not be fully realised until some time after the last project has been delivered. *Closing a programme* identifies the need for future assessment of benefit realisation as well as a formal review of those achieved so far.

16.2 Activities

16.2.1 Confirming programme closure

Programme closure may be scheduled at any point after the completion of the last project within the Project Portfolio – unless circumstances have changed, affecting the viability of the programme and causing it to be terminated earlier. To a large extent, when the programme formally closes will depend on the amount of support required to ensure the new operational environment delivered by the programme is fully embedded.

Whilst the programme is running, the programme itself is able to support and facilitate the overall change process. After closure, the embedded changes must be able to continue with smooth running operations and working practices. For programmes where the outcome primarily affects those external to the organisation running the programme, any ongoing support requirements should be established, separate from the programme, so the programme can formally close.

Programme closure involves formal confirmation that the Business Case has been satisfied, all projects have completed satisfactorily, and any remaining handover or transition activities required have been defined and assigned to relevant business operations.

If the programme is being closed prematurely (that is, before the Blueprint has been achieved), the remaining 'live' projects that are still required by the organisation need to be reassigned to business management or perhaps to another programme.

16.2.2 Programme review

Throughout the programme, the end-of-tranche reviews will have been monitoring and measuring benefits realisation. As part of programme closure a formal review should be conducted to assess the delivery of the complete Blueprint and realisation of the overall benefits.

This review should also assess and evaluate the performance of the programme and its management processes to identify lessons learned that may benefit other programmes. The review may involve independent external scrutiny, such as a Gateway Review.

A further review, following programme closure, may be required to provide a complete assessment of benefits realised as a result of the programme, including those benefits that may not have been ready for measurement and assessment when the programme closed. To reinforce the work of the programme, a continuous improvement philosophy should be established such that the organisation is able to encourage further improvements in performance.

16.2.3 Update and finalise programme information

Programme information should be reviewed and updated to ensure any remaining issues, risks, and outstanding actions have been dealt with appropriately.

16.2.4 Disband Programme Management Team and support functions

The programme's infrastructure and management processes are disbanded and individuals and resources released from the programme. Staff redeployment back into the organisation should be planned in advance. Staff will have updated their skills as a result of their experiences on the programme, and it is important that this is reflected in their personal development information. Any contracts used by the programme should be finalised and closed, or responsibility for continued

contract management handed over to the relevant business management function.

16.2.5 Inform stakeholders

The Senior Responsible Owner and the Sponsoring Group confirm programme closure. All stakeholders should be informed of programme closure and its outcome.

16.3 Inputs, outputs and decisions

Table 16.1 summarises the inputs, outputs and decisions associated with *Closing a programme*.

16.4 Responsibilities

Table 16.2 summarises the responsibilities for the activities involved in *Closing a programme*.

Table 16.1 Inputs, outputs and decisions for *Closing a programme*

Item	Type	Notes
All programme information	Input	Reviewed, updated as necessary and formally closed and filed
Confirmation of programme closure	Output	Formal notification to stakeholders of programme closure
Review	Output	Assessment of the overall performance of the programme. Further reviews for measuring realisation of benefits are scheduled
Lessons learned and programme assessment	Output	To inform future programmes

Table 16.2 Roles and responsibilities for *Closing a programme*

Role	Responsibilities
Business Change Manager	Performance assessment, measurement of benefits realised and establishing any ongoing measurement processes
Programme Manager	Finalisation of programme information, disbanding the programme team and releasing programme resources
Programme Office	Closure of programme information and setting up future review requirements
Sponsoring Group	Confirmation for sign-off for programme closure and release of Senior Responsible Owner
Senior Responsible Owner	Leading the reviews, release of personnel and sign-off for programme closure

4 Glossary and appendices

This Part provides a glossary of terms and
appendices covering:

- programme information – describing the
typical contents of documentation used
to plan and manage a programme

- the case for Programme Management –
providing some of the benefits of using
the approach

- a risk management checklist – a useful
checklist for assisting risk identification

- performance management – a summary
of techniques supporting performance
management

- differences between projects and
programmes.

17 Glossary of terms

This glossary includes terms introduced within this guide and others that are relevant to Programme Management. Many of these terms are also used in a more general sense; the definitions included here are the specific ones used within the discipline of Programme Management.

assurance	Independent assessment and confirmation that the programme as a whole or any of its aspects are on track, applying relevant practices and procedures, and that the projects, activities and business rationale remain aligned to the programme's objectives
benefit	The quantifiable and measurable improvement resulting from an outcome which is perceived as positive by a stakeholder and which will normally have a tangible value expressed in monetary or resource terms. Benefits are expected when a change is conceived. Benefits are realised as a result of activities undertaken to effect the change
Benefit Profile	The complete description of a benefit or dis-benefit
Benefits Realisation Plan	A complete view of all the Benefit Profiles in the form of a schedule
benefits management	A continuous management process running throughout the programme. It provides the programme with a target and a means of monitoring achievement against that target on a regular basis
Benefits Management Strategy	How the programme will handle benefits management
Blueprint	A model of the business or organisation, its working practices and processes, the information it requires and the technology that will be needed to deliver the capability described in the Vision Statement
Business Case	A document aggregating the specific programme information on overall costs, the anticipated benefit realisation, the timeframe, and the risk profile of the programme
Business Case Management	The manner in which the programme's rationale, objectives, benefits and risks are balanced against the financial investment, and this balance maintained, adjusted and assessed during the programme
Business Change Manager	The role responsible for benefits management, from identification through to delivery, and ensuring the implementation and embedding of the new capabilities delivered by the projects. Typically allocated to more than one individual. Alternative title: 'Change Agent'

capability	A service, function or operation that enables the organisation to exploit opportunities
Change Agent	*See* Business Change Manager
Communications Plan	A plan of the communications activities during the programme
cross-organisational programme	A programme requiring the committed involvement of more than one organisation to achieve the desired outcomes. Also referred to as 'cross-cutting' programmes
dependency network	A representation of all the inputs and outputs from the projects and how they interrelate, treating each project as a 'black box'
dis-benefit	An unwanted result of an outcome; the negative quantification of an outcome
end goal	The ultimate objective of a programme
Gateway Review	A formal and independent review of the programme (or project) providing assurance on whether the programme is operating effectively and is likely to achieve its outcomes
governance (as used in this guide)	The functions, responsibilities, processes and procedures that define how the programme is set up, managed and controlled
issue	A problem, query, concern or change request that affects the programme and requires management intervention and action to resolve
Issue Log	The log of all issues raised during the programme
Issue Resolution Strategy	How the programme will handle issue resolution
outcome	The result of change, normally affecting real-world behaviour and/or circumstances. Outcomes are desired when a change is conceived. Outcomes are achieved as a result of the activities undertaken to effect the change
portfolio management	The co-ordination of a number of projects
product	Any input or output that can be identified and described in a tangible or measurable way
programme	A portfolio of projects and activities that are co-ordinated and managed as a unit such that they achieve outcomes and realise benefits
Programme Board	A group or committee that may be established to assist with the direction-setting and leadership of a programme. The Sponsoring Group may form a Programme Board

Programme Brief	An outline description of the programme's objectives, desired benefits, risks, costs and timeframe
Programme Definition	The collection of information defining the programme covering: Vision Statement, Blueprint, Business Case, organisation structure, Project Portfolio, Benefit Profiles, Stakeholder Map
Programme Director	The title previously used for the role with ultimate accountability for the programme – 'Senior Responsible Owner' is the title used in this guide
Programme Management	The co-ordinated organisation, direction and implementation of a portfolio of projects and activities that together achieve outcomes and realise benefits that are of strategic importance
Programme Manager	The role responsible for the set-up, management and delivery of the programme. Typically allocated to a single individual
Programme Mandate	The trigger for the programme from senior management who are sponsoring the programme
Programme Office	The function providing the information hub for the programme and its delivery objectives
programme organisation	How the programme will be managed throughout its lifecycle, the roles and responsibilities of individuals involved in the programme, and personnel management or Human Resources arrangements
Programme Plan	A comprehensive document scheduling the projects, their costs, resources, risks, and transition activities together with monitoring and control activities
project	A particular way of managing activities to deliver specific outputs over a specified period and within cost, quality and resource constraints
Project Portfolio	A list of all the projects and activities that together will deliver the required 'future state' described in the Blueprint and hence achieve the capabilities expressed in the Vision Statement
Quality Management Strategy	How the programme will achieve the required levels of quality in the way the programme is managed and directed, and how the programme's deliverables will be assessed for 'fitness for purpose'
Resource Management Strategy	Description of the resource requirements for the programme and how they will be managed
Risk	A negative threat (or potential positive opportunity) that might affect the course of the programme

Risk Log	*See* Risk Register
Risk Management Strategy	How the programme will establish and maintain an effective risk management regime on the programme
Risk Register	The log of all risks identified during the programme. Often called the 'Risk Log'
role	A particular set of responsibilities and accountabilities that may be allocated to one or more individuals. In some circumstances, roles may be merged together as long as there is no conflict of interest
Senior Responsible Owner	The title given to the individual who is ultimately accountable for successful delivery, that is, the successful achievement of desired outcomes and realisation of expected benefits from a programme. This role was previously referred to as 'Programme Director'
Sponsoring Group	Senior level sponsorship of the programme providing the investment decision and top-level endorsement of the rationale and objectives for the programme. May be known as 'Programme Board'
stakeholder	An individual, group of organisation with an interest in, or influence over, the programme
Stakeholder Management Strategy	How the programme will identify and analyse the stakeholders and how ongoing communications will be achieved between the programme and all its stakeholders
Stakeholder Map	A matrix showing stakeholders and their particular interests in the programme
tranche	A group of projects structured around distinct step changes in capability and benefit delivery
value management	A management technique to define the perceived and actual value to the organisation, and then assessing progress and achievements based on this value
Vision Statement	An outward-facing description of the new capabilities resulting from programme delivery

Appendix A The case for Programme Management

Programme Management is a management framework covering organisation, processes and governance. Programme Management brings related projects and activities together in order to manage their relationships. It maintains a strategic view over the work, in order to align and co-ordinate it in support of specific business strategies. It provides the link that connects individual projects to a rapidly changing business environment and often a constantly evolving strategy.

Table A.1 summarises some of the benefits of using Programme Management.

Programme Management provides a structure and set of processes to ensure that:

- outcomes for high-level policies and strategies are identified and managed through to successful delivery

- links are made between the top-level strategic direction of organisations and the management activities required to achieve strategic objectives

- management focuses attention clearly on the delivery of outcomes and realisation of benefits that are defined and understood at the outset and achieved throughout the lifetime of the programme and beyond

- the goals of a programme remain valid in response to changes outside the programme

- all stakeholders are informed and involved and their interests are appropriately considered

- senior managers are able to plan and control activities, set priorities and allocate resources for implementation of groups of related projects

- the impact of changes on the organisations and stakeholders involved is managed and the intended change is achieved in the optimum way

- the effective delegation and management of work is executed through discrete projects and related activities

- all issues are recognised and managed to increase the chances for success

- risks to the programme's successful completion are identified, monitored, managed and controlled in a way acceptable to management

- increases the probability that change will be delivered under visible control, increases the probability of realisation of desired benefits.

A Programme Management approach should be applied flexibly and with different emphasis to suit the nature and particular needs of the programme. In all cases, however, the approach should add value to the work of the projects involved. Managing the programme should be about delivering more than just the 'sum of the parts' through the co-ordination, alignment, communication, planning and risk management activities of the programme team.

Table A.1 The benefits of Programme Management

Area of impact	Benefits of using Programme Management
Delivery of change	More effective delivery of changes because they can be planned and implemented in an integrated way, ensuring that current business operations are not adversely affected
Alignment between strategy and project levels	Effective response to strategic initiatives by bridging the gap between strategies and projects
Management support	Keeping activities focused on the business change objectives by providing a framework for senior management to direct and manage the change process
Resource management	More efficient management of resources by providing a mechanism for project prioritisation and project integration
Risk management	Better management of risk because the wider context is understood and explicitly acknowledged
Benefit realisation	Helping to achieve real business benefits through a formal process of benefit identification, management, realisation and measurement
Budgetary control	Improved control through a framework within which the costs of introducing new infrastructure, standards and quality regimes can be justified, measured and assessed
Improved performance	Clarification of how new business operations will deliver improved performance by defining the desired benefits and linking these to the achievement of new working practices
Management of Business Case	More effective management of the Business Case by building and maintaining a Business Case that clearly compares current business operations with the more beneficial future business operations
Co-ordination and control	More efficient co-ordination and control of the often complex range of activities by clearly defining roles and responsibilities for managing the Project Portfolio and realising the benefits expected from the programme
Transition management	Smooth transition from current to future business operations through the clear recognition and responsibility for preparing the organisation for migration to new ways of working
Consistency	Achieving a consistent system of new or amended policies, standards, and working practices through the integrated definition, planning, delivery and assurance of the required changes

Appendix B Programme information

Title and purpose	Typical contents	Role responsible for document	Derivation
Benefit Profile Used to define each benefit (and dis-benefit) and track its realisation	Description of the benefit (or dis-benefit) Interdependencies with other benefits When the benefit is expected to occur and over what period of time realisation will take place Measure for the realisation of the benefit and how it will be carried out; the 'before' state measurement; financial valuations wherever possible Key performance indicators in the business operations that will be affected by the benefit, immediately after realisation and for the future, and current or baseline performance levels. This may be achieved through the measurement of a single benefit or of a group of benefits Details of the changes required to the current business processes and operations in order for the benefit to be realised Costs associated with realisation and measurement Project(s) within the programme directly related to the realisation of the benefit Any dependencies on risks or other programmes or projects Individual responsible for realisation of the benefit and who will 'own' the Benefit Profile during the programme. This will typically be the relevant Business Change Manager appointed from the business area concerned	Business Change Manager	Vision Statement Blueprint

Title and purpose	Typical contents	Role responsible for document	Derivation
Benefits Realisation Plan Used to track realisation of benefits across the programme	Schedule detailing when each benefit or group of benefits will be realised Identification of appropriate milestones when a programme benefit review could be carried out Details of any handover activities, beyond the mere implementation of a deliverable or output, to sustain the process of benefits realisation after the programme is closed	Programme Manager	Benefit Profiles Programme Plan
Benefits Management Strategy Used to establish the approach to managing benefits	Outline description of the programme's benefits and where in the organisation the benefits will occur Model of the benefits showing any interdependencies and dependencies on specific areas of change required within the organisation Description of the functions, roles and responsibilities for benefit planning and realisation, aligned with the programme's organisation structure Review and assessment process for measuring benefit realisation covering: who will be involved in the reviews; how and when the reviews will be carried out	Programme Manager	Vision Statement Blueprint

Title and purpose	Typical contents	Role responsible for document	Derivation
Blueprint Used to maintain the programme's focus on delivering the required transformation and business change	Business models of functions, processes and operations, including operational costs and performance levels, of the required 'future' state Organisation structure, staffing levels, roles and skill requirements necessary to support the future business operations. Any necessary changes to organisational culture, style, or existing structures and personnel may also be included Technology, IT systems, tools, equipment, buildings and accommodation required for the future business operations together with details of reuse of existing infrastructure or implementation of new infrastructure to support the 'future' state Data and information required for the future business operations, together with details of how existing data and information will be changed or redeveloped to provide the necessary requirements for the 'future' state	Programme Manager	Programme Mandate Programme Brief Vision Statement
Business Case Used to validate the ongoing viability of the programme	Strategic objectives for the programme, reflecting the Vision Statement, and alignment with the organisational context and business environment Expected benefits or outcomes, with recognition of the organisation's capability to achieve the necessary transformation and change Overall risk profile, indicating the major risks to programme delivery and benefit realisation. Detailed risk assessment will be part of the programme's Risk Register Any assumptions that underpin the Business Case Estimated costs and overall timescales. Detailed scheduling of programme milestones will be part of the Programme Plan Investment appraisal (if appropriate)	Senior Responsible Owner	Programme Brief Vision Statement Blueprint Programme Plan Benefit Profiles

Title and purpose	Typical contents	Role responsible for document	Derivation
Communications Plan Used to plan and monitor the communication activities during the programme	Description of key messages and programme information to be communicated, and the objectives for delivering these communications Responsibilities for delivering key messages and other information about the programme Description of channels to be used Schedule of communications activities, including target audiences for each	Programme Manager	Stakeholder Management Strategy and Stakeholder Map Vision Statement Blueprint
Resource Management Strategy Used to identify the required resources and define how they will be acquired and managed	Funding requirements; accounting procedures for costs and expenditure; budgets for Programme Management resources and funding sources Cost and expenditure profile across the programme; expenditure approval procedures; financial reporting procedures Assets required, such as buildings and office equipment Staff and personnel requirements, including HR requirements for supporting staff through transition Technology and services required Profile of resources that are shared across more than one of the projects within the portfolio. This profile should indicate the expected use by each project of the shared resource within time periods	Programme Manager	Programme Plan

Title and purpose	Typical contents	Role responsible for document	Derivation
Issue Log Used to capture and actively manage programme issues	Unique reference for each issue raised, date it was raised and by whom Description of the issue and what actual or likely impact it has on the programme or projects The severity of the issue, for example, the degree to which the interests of the programme could be harmed. Categories for severity might be 'critical' (that is, adverse effect on the benefits such that continuation of the programme is unacceptable), 'major', 'significant', and 'minor' Programme Manager has overall responsibility for resolving issues, however, each issue should be assigned to an individual who is best placed to take or manage the necessary actions Current status of the issue and progress on its resolution including providing feedback to the source	Programme Manager	Issues raised during the programme
Issue Resolution Strategy Used to implement appropriate mechanisms and procedures for resolving issues	How issues will be captured and assessed, and by whom How information about their likely impact will be defined How ownership will be handled How actions will be identified and by whom; who will carry out and manage the required actions How actions will be monitored and evaluated for their effectiveness What communication mechanisms will be set up; how stakeholders will be engaged throughout the process	Programme Manager	Previous project and programmes Stakeholder Management Strategy Risk Management Strategy

Title and purpose	Typical contents	Role responsible for document	Derivation
Programme Brief Used to define the programme objectives and outcomes	Description of the capability the organisation seeks from changes to the business and/or its operations. Delivery of this capability is the end goal of the programme. The description forms an outline Vision Statement for the programme Outline description of the benefits or types of benefits that should be delivered from the new capability, an estimate of when they are likely to be achieved, and an indication of how they will be measured. It is often necessary to consider 'dis-benefits' (where one of the parties may be worse off as a result of the programme) alongside the benefits in order to present a more complete and realistic 'picture' of the programme's outcome Explanation of the risks to the programme that can be recognised at this point in time, any current issues that may affect the programme, and any known constraints, assumptions or conflicts that may potentially affect the programme. It is important to be able to balance the desired benefits arising from the programme against the risks and issues that may prevent the benefits from being fully realised As much detail as is available on the estimated costs, timescales and effort required to set up, manage and run the programme from startup through to delivery and realisation of the benefits. The overall timescale for the programme may be relatively long, perhaps two to five years. To provide an indication of the effort and resources required, an initial listing of candidate projects or activities required should be included, together with rough timescales	Senior Responsible Owner	Programme Mandate

Title and purpose	Typical contents	Role responsible for document	Derivation
Programme Mandate Used to describe the required outcomes from the programme based on strategic or policy objectives	What the programme is intended to deliver in terms of new services and/or operational capability How the organisation(s) involved will be improved as a result of delivering the new services/capability How the programme fits into the corporate mission and goals and any other initiatives that are already underway or will be underway during the lifetime of the programme	Sponsoring Group	Business strategy or policy
Programme Plan Used to design the overall programme and then to monitor and control progress	Project information including the list of projects (the Project Portfolio), their target timescales and costs, and the dependency network showing the dependencies between the projects Summary of the risks and assumptions identified against successful achievement of the Programme Plan. The programme's Risk Register contains the detailed risk assessment and associated contingency actions Overall programme schedule showing the relative sequencing of the projects, the grouping of projects into tranches, milestone review points. The schedule should also include timings of communications activities, risk mitigation actions and quality review work to be carried out at the programme level Transition plan showing when the outputs from the projects will be delivered to the business and what transition activities will be required to embed the new capability into business operations. The transition plan will need to be closely linked to the programme schedule to ensure any changes in the delivery from the projects is fed into the transition planning process Monitoring and control activities, data requirements, performance targets, and responsibilities	Programme Manager	Blueprint Benefits Management Strategy Benefit Profiles Benefits Realisation Plan Business Case Project Portfolio

Title and purpose	Typical contents	Role responsible for document	Derivation
Project Portfolio Used to define how the programme will deliver the outcome(s) and benefits	List of existing and new projects, together with any relevant workstream activity Outline information on outputs, timescales, resource requirements and dependencies with other projects Links showing what contribution each project will make to the benefits	Programme Manager	Blueprint Benefit Profiles
Quality Management Strategy Used to define and establish the activities for managing quality across the programme	Description of the quality assurance, review and control processes for the programme covering: What will be subject to quality assurance, review and control and the quality criteria to be applied Who will undertake quality assurance, review and control activities What will trigger these activities (time-based, event-based, or associated with risk occurrence) What actions will be taken depending on the results of quality checks Configuration Management and change control procedures Defined responsibilities for quality management Information requirements to support quality management Procedures for use of support tools for quality management activities, for example, change control software Resource requirements for quality management	Programme Manager	Corporate quality management systems Industry standards Programme Definition

Handwritten annotations:

adhere to governance 8hrs? →

activities — PM, SRO, BCMS, other

→ issues / risks

end of tranche; coincide with org dates

* overlap but not nec the same — might be responsible but not undertake or vice versa

Prog office likely to do lot of the work

Title and purpose	Typical contents	Role responsible for document	Derivation
Risk Management Strategy Used to define and establish the required activities and responsibilities for managing the programme's risks	How risks will be identified and quantified How information about their probability and impact will be defined How risk ownership will be handled How responses and actions will be identified How decisions on risk management will be made, and by whom, for example, tolerance levels How these decisions will be implemented How actions will be monitored and evaluated for their effectiveness What communication mechanisms will be set up, how stakeholders will be engaged throughout the process	Programme Manager	Corporate Risk Management Strategy Previous projects and programmes

Title and purpose	Typical contents	Role responsible for document	Derivation
Risk Register Used to capture and actively manage the programme risks	Unique reference for each risk identified. This reference may need to be reflected in project-level Risk Registers when the risk could impact on one or more projects as well as the programme Description of the risk to the programme and which projects are likely to have an impact on the risk (either increasing its likelihood, or reducing it) Description of the impact on the programme should the risk materialise Proximity of the risk, which is an estimation of timescale for when the risk might materialise. The accuracy of this estimation increases as the point in time approaches. The scale should provide for continuous and equal time windows that will align easily with the programme's risk management processes. For example, if the programme has a planned duration of thirty months and the Programme Management Team has agreed to meet every three months, then the proximity scale could sensibly use three-month increments Probability of realisation of the risk. This could be a mathematical calculation, or a simpler 'high, medium, low' classification Severity of the risk, for example the degree to which the interests of the programme would be harmed should the risk materialise. Categories for severity might be 'critical' (that is, adverse effect on the benefits such that continuation of the programme is unacceptable), 'major', 'significant', and 'minor' Risk owner – the Programme Manager has overall responsibility for managing programme risks; however, each risk should be assigned to the individual who is best placed to monitor it and manage any necessary actions Response to the risk, which reduces either the probability of the risk happening or its effects, should it happen Current status of the risk itself and progress of any actions relating to the management of the risk	Programme Manager	Blueprint Benefit Profiles Benefits Realisation Plan Business Case Project Portfolio Programme Plan

Title and purpose	Typical contents	Role responsible for document	Derivation
Stakeholder Management Strategy Used to define and implement the objectives, activities and responsibilities for managing stakeholders	List of all stakeholders, appropriately grouped Analysis of influence and impact for each stakeholder group Stakeholder Map showing the different stakeholder interests in the programme Description of how the programme will engage with all stakeholders including mechanisms for encouraging, receiving and responding to feedback from stakeholders Measures to determine how well the communication process is engaging with stakeholders	Programme Manager	Vision Statement Blueprint
Stakeholder Map Used to model stakeholder interests	Matrix showing each stakeholder or stakeholder group against their interest areas in the programme	Programme Manager	Vision Statement Blueprint
Vision Statement Used to communicate the end goal of the programme	Clear statement of the 'end goal' of the programme Supported by a description of the new or changed capabilities together with performance measures or service levels indicating the desired improvements resulting from programme delivery	Senior Responsible Owner	Programme Mandate Programme Brief

Appendix C Risk identification checklist

The following checklist of questions may be helpful when identifying potential risks to the programme.

C.1 Strategic level risks

- What are the risks emerging from the environment in which the business operates and the environment in which programmes are run?

- What is the risk to the business if the programme succeeds or fails?

- Has the organisation the capability and capacity to undertake the programme?

C.1.1 Other programmes

Existing programmes may both be a source of risk to a new programme and offer the benefit of experience for identifying risks:

- What analysis of risk has already been carried out?

- Has the analysis of risk from legacy programmes been realistically reviewed?

- What has gone wrong in the past, and what lessons can be learned from those experiences?

- Are new inter-programme dependencies created?

C.1.2 Other initiatives within the organisation

If a new initiative arises during the course of a programme, work through the impact of the new initiative on the programme.

- Is it possible to revise the programme to accommodate the new initiative?

- If not, what are the impacts of delaying the new initiative's introduction or introducing it as a separate programme?

C.1.3 Inter-programme dependencies

Although they are often difficult to anticipate, dependencies between programmes should be carefully considered.

C.1.4 Political pressures

- Are political pressures on the programme well understood and documented?

- Have they been regularly revisited through the life of the programme?

- What risks threaten successful management of the programme?

C.2 Programme-level risks

If objectives are vague the programme is likely to be exposed to considerable dangers during implementation, especially if a new initiative causes the programme's objectives to alter. Can the programme be delivered?

C.2.1 Changing requirements and objectives

- Have the sponsors reached a genuine consensus on the objectives for the programme?

- Can the objectives be quantifiably defined, so that success can be measured later?

C.2.2 Programme definition

Risk is inherent in planning a programme:

- Does the programme call for any divergence from organisational standards?

- Have the stakeholders been involved in defining and planning the programme?

- Have approval and sign-off procedures been set in place?

C.2.3 Management skills

Ensure that the logical roles identified for managing the programme are appropriately tailored and there are clear responsibilities for named individuals.

- What skills are required for the particular programme?

- Are in-house skills available?

- Are third-party providers required to assist with the management of the programme?

C.2.4 Inter-project dependencies

The Programme Manager is responsible for defining and monitoring inter-project dependencies.

- Are the interdependencies between projects clearly defined?

- What risks may affect the conduct of projects?

C.3 Project-level risks

To manage the risks to projects well, it is necessary to:

- ensure each Project Brief outlines the risks from the perspective of the programme

- provide feedback to the programme's risk analysis and management activities as individual projects progress.

C.3.1 Third-party resources

It may be expected that a lack of in-house skills can be met by bringing them in from outside. Careful thought should be given to what bundles of products and services are to be provided by third parties.

- Is there difficulty in drawing up exact terms of reference, specifications and contracts?

- Can win-win relationships be established with service providers, or are they likely to be adversarial?

- Is there pressure to contract out core management tasks?

- Has enough time been allowed for procurement of external resources?

- Is the management of third parties and the associated contract management function understood and resourced?

C.4 Operational-level risks

Transition must be properly planned, managed and resourced. There may be projects required to achieve 'soft' deliverables (for example, changes in staff behaviour) as well as physical outputs. Will new ways of working introduce new risks, such as fraud or abuse of financial arrangements?

C.4.1 Transfer of outputs to operations

- Are there constraints that limit proper piloting and testing?

- Are expectations realistic?

- What risks arise from handing over project outputs to the business and bringing in change with new systems or new ways of working?

C.4.2 Acceptability within business operations

Business managers must be involved in the benefits identification and management processes.

- Have the relevant business managers been identified, and whose areas will be affected by the outcome of the programme?

- How are they involved in identifying and realising the benefits to the business through improved performance of their operations?

C.4.3 Acceptability to stakeholders

The same considerations apply to the programme's stakeholders.

- Are stakeholders' requirements understood and reflected in the programme's aims and objectives?

- Are the stakeholders suitably involved within the programme?

Appendix D Performance measurement

The following techniques may be useful to support performance measurement on a programme. The 'Further information' section includes references to other guidance on performance management.

D.1 Goal Question Metric

The Goal Question Metric technique is based on the assumptions that in order to measure performance:

- goals need to be defined

- goals need to be related to data that will track performance against them

- a framework is needed to interpret the data with respect to the goals.

Goals can be associated with products, processes and/or resources. Questions are developed to focus on the achievement of some performance or quality aspect of each goal. Metrics are defined, associating a set of data with every question in order to answer it in a quantitative way.

D.2 Balanced scorecard

The balanced scorecard technique provides a structured approach to the use of performance measurement techniques in the setting of goals and objectives, and translating the organisation's strategy into performance measures and targets. The balanced scorecard is based on the principle that a balanced mix of measures is necessary to represent adequately the breadth of corporate performance. The measures should represent the views of all stakeholders and also strike a balance between these types of measures:

- financial and non-financial measures

- external measures, which are of concern to stakeholders and customers, and internal measures, which address business processes, innovation and growth

- outcome measures, which look at the results of previous activities, and the measures that will have most impact on future performance.

D.3 EFQM Excellence Model

The Excellence Model defines a framework for business improvement and the measurement of that improvement. The model is widely used in both the public and private sectors, in the UK and internationally. A major advantage of the model is that it provides a common framework and terminology for people from different organisations to compare processes and practices.

The model consists of a set of criteria against which the organisation can be assessed. The criteria fall into two categories:

- enablers: factors that assess the organisation's readiness and capability to achieve business improvement

- results: comparison with targets and trends.

The model also incorporates innovation and learning, which take the form of feedback from results to enablers.

D.4 Benchmarking

Benchmarking is a management technique to improve business performance. It is used to compare performance between different organisations, or different units within a single organisation, undertaking similar processes, on a continuous basis. It can be used to:

- assess performance objectively

- expose areas where improvement is needed

- identify other organisations with processes resulting in superior performance, with a view to their adoption

- test whether improvement programmes have been successful.

Three main types of benchmarking can be distinguished:

- **standards** benchmarking – this involves setting a standard of performance which an effective organisation could be expected to achieve. Information on the organisation's performance against the standard can be used as a monitoring tool

- **results** benchmarking – this compares the performance of a number of organisations providing a similar service. In the absence of competitive pressures, this can provide a significant incentive to improve efficiency

- **process** benchmarking – this involves undertaking a detailed examination within a group of organisations of the processes which produce a particular output, with a view to understanding the reasons for variations in performance and incorporating best practice.

Appendix E Differences between programmes and projects

Projects tend to have definite start and finish points, with the aim of delivering a predetermined output, giving them relatively clear development paths from initiation to delivery. Programmes, on the other hand, typically have a more strategic vision of the desired end goal, but no clearly defined path to get there. Programmes are able to deal with the uncertainty surrounding the achievement of the vision, whereas projects work best where the outputs can be well defined.

Programmes are about managing change. They typically involve changes to culture and work practices as well as changes to business operations and services. Changing cultures and styles of management takes time. Programmes can embrace the management and leadership of culture change because they typically have longer timeframes than projects.

Benefits accrue at the end of a project, after the output has been delivered. In contrast, a programme will co-ordinate the delivery from a set of projects such that benefits can be realised within the timescales of the programme as well as afterwards. A programme is likely

Table E.1 Some typical differences between projects and programmes

Managing project delivery	Managing programmes
An intense and focused activity that is concerned with delivering predetermined outputs	A broadly spread activity concerned with delivering business change objectives and achieving outcomes, realising a wider set of benefits than the individual projects could realise in isolation
Is best suited to closely bounded and scoped deliverables that can be relatively well defined	Suited to activities with complex and changing inter-relationships in a wider, more dynamic and uncertain environment
Realises benefits following the end of the project, after implementation of the project's outputs	Realises benefits both during and after conclusion of the programme, having put in place mechanisms for measuring the improvements in business performance
	Suited to managing benefits realisation and ensuring a smooth and risk-reduced transition into a new business operation
	Able to maintain 'business as usual' in areas affected by the change whilst managing the transition to new operations
	Usually continues until the organisation has achieved the required outcomes (a programme may of course be stopped earlier if it is no longer valid)

to include some projects that do not directly produce benefits but are nonetheless essential to delivering the overall programme benefits.

Relative timescales are also a way of differentiating between a project and a programme. Projects typically have a shorter timeframe for completion than programmes. Projects will usually be measured in months; programmes will often be measured in years.

The ways in which projects and programmes are managed also demonstrate that a project is different from a programme. Some typical differences between managing project delivery and managing programmes are shown in Table E.1.

not all projects in programme → benefits

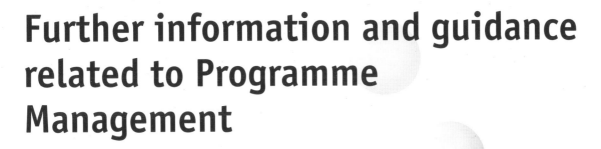

Further information and guidance related to Programme Management

Office of Government Commerce (OGC)

OGC has developed a wide range of high-level guidance covering strategy, Programme Management, service management, procurement and performance management.

Details of OGC guidance (including the OGC Gateway process) may be found in the OGC Successful Delivery Toolkit at www.ogc.gov.uk/sdtoolkit, or from:

The OGC Service Desk
Rosebery Court
St Andrews Business Park
Norwich NR7 0HS
Telephone: + 44 (0) 845 000 4999
Email: ServiceDesk@ogc.gov.uk
Website: http://www.ogc.gov.uk

Details about the OGC Successful Delivery Skills programme, which includes Programme Management, can be found at www.sds.ogc.gov.uk (see below for specific training and qualifications for Managing Successful Programmes).

Accredited training and professional qualifications

The APM Group Ltd, on behalf of OGC, administers the accredited training scheme and professional qualifications for Managing Successful Programmes. Full details of all accredited training providers are available on request.

APM Group Ltd
7–8 Queen Square
High Wycombe
Buckinghamshire HP11 2BP
Telephone: (01494) 452450
Fax: (01494) 459559
Website: http://www.programmes.org/

OGC guidance published by partners

A complete catalogue of all OGC guidance can be obtained from the OGC Service Desk or from our publishing partners Format Publishing (www.formatpublishing.co.uk) and TSO (www.tso.co.uk). The following publications have direct relevance to Managing Successful Programmes:

Management of Risk: Guidance for Practitioners
ISBN 0-11-330909-0
Published by TSO

Managing Successful Projects with PRINCE2
ISBN 0-11-330891-4
Published by TSO

How to Manage Business Change
ISBN 1-90-309110-1
Published by Format Publishing

How to Manage Performance
ISBN 1-90-309113-6
Published by Format Publishing

Business Benefits through Project Management
ISBN 0-11-330898-1
Published by TSO

Index

References to tables are shown in *italic*, and figures in **bold**. Terms included in the glossary are indicated by the letter 'g' after the page reference.